ENDORSEMI

"Every Christian will benefit from this book! It is filled with principles that will challenge your prayer life and encourage your pastor. If you long to see God at work in transformational ways in your church, begin with applying the biblical truths in *Pit Crew: Praying Our Pastors Will Finish*. Buy one book for yourself and ten more to give away!"

CAROL KENT
Speaker and Author
Waiting Together: Hope and Healing
for Families of Prisoners

"As far as I know, Sally is the first layperson to address the issue of praying for our pastors in writing. Her insightful look at the issues pastors and their families face and her burden to pray come through in a loving way. Sally uses a number of stories and examples from other peoples' lives, as well as biblical references.

Having been a pastor's wife for many years, and now sitting under the ministry of a young man my husband mentored, I can honestly say that Sally has hit on the most important issue. A lay person can do nothing more important than to pray for those who minister to him or her. It's biblical, and the bigger the 'pit crew,' the better!"

LORNA DOBSON
Speaker and Author
I'm More Than the Pastor's Wife:
Authentic Living in a Fishbowl World
Caring for Your Pastor: Helping Your Pastor Serve with Joy

"As I read Sally's book, I felt I wasn't worthy of the respect and love she shows to the role of pastor, but I knew in my soul that I desire the heart-felt and loving prayers she espouses. Serving in my calling is a privilege, and serving those that will esteem our responsibilities with the power of prayer is the church's only hope to remain light in the darkness. May God speak to our hearts as to how we may encourage one another as long as it is called today."

MARK CHRISTIAN
Senior Minister
Christ's Church of Oronogo
Oronogo, Missouri

PIT CREW

PIT CREW

PRAYING OUR PASTORS WILL FINISH THE RACE

Sally U. Smith

NASHVILLE

NEW YORK • LONDON • MELBOURNE • VANCOUVER

PIT CREW

Praying Our Pastors Will Finish the Race

Published in New York, New York, by Morgan James Publishing. Morgan James is a trademark of Morgan James, LLC. www.MorganJamesPublishing.com

The Morgan James Speakers Group can bring authors to your live event. For more information or to book an event visit The Morgan James Speakers Group at www.TheMorganJamesSpeakersGroup.com.

All Scripture quotations, unless otherwise indicated, are taken from the Holy Bible, New International Version®, niv ®. Copyright ©1973, 1978, 1984, 2011 by Biblica, Inc. Used by permission of Zondervan. All rights reserved worldwide. www.zondervan.com. The "niv" and "New International Version" are trademarks registered in the United States Patent and Trademark Office by Biblica, Inc.

Scripture quotations marked (nasb) are taken from the New American Standard Bible®, Copyright © 1960, 1962, 1963, 1968, 1971, 1972, 1973, 1975, 1977, 1995 by The Lockman Foundation. Used by permission.

Permission is granted to readers to copy up to 100 copies of the prayer lists in the Appendix for noncommercial use. Copies must contain the copyright line given in the Appendix.

ISBN 9781614488231 paperback
ISBN 9781614488248 eBook
Library of Congress Control Number: 2017910262

Cover Design by:
Rachel Lopez
www.r2cdesign.com

Interior Design by:
Chris Treccani
www.3dogcreative.net

COVER PHOTO: Anthony Zampella of Blackwater Photo Haus

In an effort to support local communities, raise awareness and funds, Morgan James Publishing donates a percentage of all book sales for the life of each book to Habitat for Humanity Peninsula and Greater Williamsburg.

Get involved today! Visit
www.MorganJamesBuilds.com

DEDICATION

To my parents, who modeled prayer
To my pastors, who taught me the Word of God

TABLE OF CONTENTS

ACKNOWLEDGEMENTS

I'd like to acknowledge some dear people for their encouragement and help in bringing this book to publication. I am grateful to all of you.

Several pastors allowed me to interview them and gave permission to quote them in *Pit Crew*. These interviews gave me insight into what our clergy face. You will read their comments soon. Tiffany and her team at Morgan James Publishing answered all of my questions.

I appreciate the fantastic editing job by Larry Wilson. Rebecca Thesman is a great friend and my proofreader. Thanks to my daughter Ely who helped me with ideas for the illustrations. Kim, my talented niece helped with photography.

No book on prayer can be written without people praying for the author. I was blessed with five prayer warriors who are too humble to let me list their names.

My duties as a mom were curtailed by the writing of this book. My family took up much of the slack for me by eating fast food and TV dinners. Thanks also to my friend Kim, who cleaned my house.

My dear writing friends at Christian Writers' Fellowship - Girard, who live in the states of Kansas, Missouri, Arkansas, and Oklahoma, were invaluable in offering professional advice and understanding the many ups and downs of an author. A special thank you goes to my critique group, consisting of: Jena, Barbara, Lindsey, Sandy, and Bonnie.

Most of all, I thank God for the opportunity to share my passion to pray for our pastors. Serving Him remains the most awesome thing I have ever done.

INTRODUCTION

I originally entitled this book *Pit Crew: Praying Our Pastors Will Finish Victoriously*. Only a few pages into the book, I changed it to *Pit Crew: Praying Our Pastors Will Finish*. This may seem like an unnecessary change to some. However, I think the renaming is important. First, the new title aligns with Scripture, (2 Timothy 4:7, "I have fought the good fight, I have finished the race, I have kept the faith").

Also, God does not call our ministers to be popular and well known, to become an author/speaker, or a blogger, radio personality, newspaper columnist, televangelist, or to have the church with the largest attendance. Our Lord calls clergy and, in fact, all believers to follow him in obedience and be faithful in using our gifts for Christ.

In the same way, God didn't call me to write a best-seller but to be faithful in writing a book to equip Christians to become intercessors and to pray regularly for their pastors.

In this book, I use NASCAR as a metaphor. This may seem odd since motor racing, like all sports, is about winning. However, this book is not about competition. Instead, I employ NASCAR to illustrate how a team works. Teams finish the race.

A driver flies across the finish line only because a great pit crew worked hard both on and off the track. In our churches, the pastor finishes the race only when people in the pews intercede to push the pastor across the finish line of his or her God-given ministry.

One example of this is Richard Perry Ellis, who recently passed to his heavenly reward at age eighty-four. Ellis pastored seven churches in four states before serving as a missionary in Brazil from 1970 to 1984. At a towering six feet nine inches tall, he preached about missions in nine countries. Ellis's final pastorate was a church plant in his independent living facility, where he preached weekly until the day before his death.[1] He kept the faith.

You may also wonder about the title of this series, Pray to Win. Doesn't the series name imply a striving to become victorious? No, I don't mean win in that sense at all. Pray to Win proposes that we pray and then watch *God* win.

God triumphs over packed schedules. God triumphs over criticism. God triumphs over discouragement. God triumphs over whatever Satan can dream up to get our pastors out of the race.

Jesus said, "If you believe, you will receive whatever you ask for in prayer" (Matthew 21:22). Our responsibility after praying becomes trusting God to answer. He is able and desires to answer because he loves us. Our job is to pray, then anticipate his answer.

Psalm 5:3 says, "In the morning, LORD, you hear my voice; in the morning I lay my requests before you and wait expectantly."

Please become a member of your minister's pit crew. Place your high-octane petitions before the Lord and watch God propel your pastor over the finish line of his or her ministry.

1

Pastoral Responsibility

Finish with Teamwork

WINNING WISDOM

Air is not more necessary to the lungs than
prayer is to the preacher.

E. M. BOUNDS

When Dave passed the well-lit billboard, he wished he could go to the track. The sign displayed colorful corporate logos painted on streamlined stock cars. He was an avid NASCAR fan but could not find the time to go to a race. In fact, he could not recall the last time he watched a race on television. The sound of an engine screaming around a corner, the smell of tires after a burnout, and the taste of buttery concession popcorn were fond memories.

Dave's favorite part of the race was the pit stop. An efficient pit crew will win the race for its beloved driver. Dave watched the seven over-the-wall guys leap the pit row barrier and dash into action. The tires were changed, the gas tank was filled, and the windshield was cleaned. A long pole was extended so the driver could sip a bottle of Gatorade.[2]

The whole event took about fifteen seconds. Most races required eight pit stops. Dave felt the pit crew members were the unsung heroes of the race team.[3]

I wish I had a pit crew! he thought, *Someone to take the pressure off all the responsibility I face in ministry.*

As Dave pulled into his empty garage, a wave of exhaustion from the lengthy board meeting swept over his body. Dave's two-story house stood dark and silent. He plodded to the master bath and closed the door carefully so as not to wake his wife. After Dave changed into his sleep pants, he glanced at his cell phone to check the calendar. His first appointment was scheduled for ten the next morning. Dave fell into bed, glad for the chance to get a little extra sleep before returning to work.

At six o'clock the next morning, the phone startled Dave awake.

"Pastor Dave, this is Rich Stinson. Megan didn't come home last night after the ball game. We called all of her friends. They said their gang went to the game and then out for pizza. The girls thought she drove straight home from the restaurant."

Dave rubbed his eyes then reached for his glasses. "Oh dear." He tried to think of something more comforting, but his mind remained anesthetized with sleep.

"We called the police and the hospital to see if there had been an accident. Now, the police are asking questions about her running away. I don't know if they think she has or if they are just covering all of the bases. Mary and I don't know what to do. Can you get the church leadership together to pray?"

"Rich, can you get Mary on the phone? I'd like to pray with both of you now, and then I'll give the others a call."

After he hung up, Dave called the chairman of the church board. The Stinsons were members of his small group, and he was eager to help. He arranged a leader's prayer group with a continental breakfast at his home.

As the board members prayed, Dave's cell phone vibrated. He left the room to take the call. His wife, Janet, spoke with urgency. "Sweetheart, I just received a call from Ken Wilson. His wife fell and is being taken by ambulance to the ER with a possible broken hip."

Dave excused himself from the prayer group, drove to the hospital, and waited for the x-ray results with Ken Wilson, an elderly man from the church. While there, Dave took calls from his secretary, scheduled a missionary to speak at the church, and ordered Sunday school curriculum. Then the board chairman called with an offer to meet for lunch at the mall deli to pray for Megan's return. A doctor came and confirmed Mrs. Wilson's hip was fractured. Dave sighed heavily when Ken's eyes erupted with tears, then they joined Ken's wife in the ER. As Dave prayed with the Wilsons, his phone sounded a notification for his ten o'clock appointment.

Dave rushed to his office for a counseling session with a couple who had separated. The wife arrived ten minutes late, and the husband didn't show. After a short session with the wife, Dave sank into his chair for daily devotions.

In the middle of the desk, Dave noticed a yellow sticky note that read, "Column due today at noon to be printed in the Gazette's Saturday religion section." He flipped the sticky note in the direction of the trash can, then searched his laptop for a recent sermon that could be converted to the required word length. Half an hour later,

Dave pressed send on his email to the editor and slumped back into his chair to return to Bible reading.

His cell phone chirped again. "Honey, can you pick up a prescription for Josh?" The doctor had diagnosed their four-year-old with strep throat.

"I don't have time," Dave snapped.

"Well . . . Josh's fever is so high, I don't think I should take him to the drug store. I guess I could get one of the ladies in my Bible study to go."

"No, I'll go through the drive-through on my way to the mall."

While Dave waited, the warning light on the dash signaled low fuel. He figured he could get to the mall and then locate a gas station.

When he got to the deli, Dave could not locate a single board member. *Great. The second time I got stood up today.* He phoned the chairman.

"Oh, I meant the deli at the strip mall. I'm so sorry."

Tool Box

In June 2004, Rusty Wallace, NASCAR driver from St. Louis, ran out of fuel on the final lap, which cost him a top-five finish.[4]

Prayer: Pray your pastor will not run out of fuel, but will run the race in the power of the Holy Spirit.

Scriptures: "Be filled with the Spirit" (Ephesians 5:18). "We live by the Spirit" *(Galatians 5:25).*

On the way back across town, Dave dropped off the antibiotic for his son, then headed for a gas station. While he waited for the gas pump to fill his late model Ford, Dave realized he had missed his opportunity to eat a sandwich from the refrigerator or grab a snack from the pantry at home. By the time he arrived at the strip mall, lunch would be over and probably most of the prayer time.

Exhausted, Dave leaned on the gas pump. The cadence of the scrolling numbers triggered a thought. He envisioned a personal gas gauge that measured his energy level. The needle pointed to the top hash of the red E. *How do I get filled up? I wish I had a pit crew.*

Pastor Dave, like the apostle Paul, wants to proclaim 2 Timothy 4:7, "I have fought the good fight, I have finished the race, I have kept the faith." Yet Dave's continued exhaustion and frustration could initiate an early exit. He requires help to stay in the race.

—•—

In the racing world, making a trip to the winner's circle necessitates a team approach among driver, mechanics, pit crew, sponsors, and owner. A team approach could benefit Dave—and all pastors. They need prayer warriors to sustain them to the finish line.

To assist you as you pray your pastor to the finish line, this book will challenge you in six areas:

1. To pray for your pastor from a motivation of love.
2. To increase your knowledge of what a pastor faces.
3. To learn invaluable prayer methods and tips.
4. To submit yourself as an instrument God can use to renew and revive your church.
5. To allow your personal walk with God to be transformed.
6. To learn how to start and lead a prayer group.

Our Expectations

Many of us experience tough weeks of disruptions, deadlines, disasters, disappointments, and dizzying activities. We look forward to Sunday to get answers and encouragement from our pastors so we can tackle the next week.

We expect our pastors to deliver a sermon that instructs and inspires us for the next leg of the journey. We need their leadership and wisdom to show us the way. We await golden nuggets of grace and truth in their messages.

Pit to Pulpit

In 2017 Barna reported that 76 percent of pastors say they know at least one fellow pastor whose ministry has ended in the last five years due to burnout or stress-related problems.[5]

Prayer: Pray that your pastor will have the strength to endure and finish the race.

Scripture: "But those who hope in the LORD will renew their strength. They will soar on wings like eagles; they will run and not grow weary, they will walk and not be faint" *(Isaiah 40:31).*

But if continual disturbances have devastated their week, how can they squeeze in time to prepare a challenge for us in our walk with the Lord? To discern the congregation's needs and to determine how to meet them effectively takes enormous skill, wisdom, and preparation. If our pastors' weeks go like Dave's morning did, they will arrive on Sunday drained and unable to communicate God's truth competently and powerfully.

Our Part

Pastors need our prayers. Our pastors are the most influential people in our spiritual development. Their sermons will not extend past the pulpit unless we intercede for them. The apostle Paul, a highly effective preacher, begged his congregation, "Brothers and sisters, pray for us" (1 Thessalonians 5:25).

Dr. Peter Wagner spent a number of years as professor of church growth at Fuller Theological Seminary. He begins his book *Prayer*

Shield by stating, "The most underutilized source of spiritual power in our churches today is intercession for Christian leaders."[6]

After serving in the Civil War, Chaplain E. M. Bounds served as an author, editor, itinerant revival minister, and prayer warrior. His daily routine involved rising at four o'clock to pray for three hours.

Bounds describes how vital it is to pray for our clergy: "Men in the pew given to praying for the preacher are like the poles which hold up the wires along which the electric current runs. They are not the power; neither are they the specific agents in making the Word of the Lord effective. But they hold up the wires, along which the divine power runs to the hearts of men."[7]

People of Passion

The best part of praying for our pastors is that it also supercharges our personal prayer life. Time spent praying for our ministers will trigger growth in three areas.[8]

Heartfelt Love

Galatians 6:2 reads, "Carry each other's burdens, and in this way you will fulfill the law of Christ." By praying for our shepherds, we help them shoulder the burden of ministry. We confirm our love for our pastors by fulfilling the greatest commandment, found in Matthew 22:34–40, the law of love.

Humility

Intercessory prayer focuses on the needs of others. Intercession develops humility in our lives.

God promises tremendous power and blessing to the humble: "All of you, clothe yourselves with humility toward one another, because, 'God opposes the proud but shows favor to the humble.'

Humble yourselves, therefore, under God's mighty hand, that he may lift you up in due time" (1 Peter 5:5–6).

Harmony

As we pray for our pastors, we become an instrument that allows the Spirit to move through us. By praying from our pastors' perspectives, we unite through the Spirit with their missions. We will see and feel the power of prayer as the truth flows from our preachers transformed lives. We will value and trust our pastors. And our shepherds will feel appreciated.

J. Lee Simmons, founder and president of Missio Global Ministries Inc., once said, "The kindest thing a person can say to me is, 'Pastor I pray for you every day.'"

Our churches will flourish when both members and ministers are praying for and serving each other.

2

Permeated with Scripture

Race Plan

WINNING WISDOM

Is prayer your steering wheel or your spare tire?

Corrie ten Boom

H endrick Motorsports is a racing team that employs over 500 people to keep four drivers on the track. In 2017 their drivers were Jimmie Johnson, Chase Elliott, Kasey Kahne, and Dale Earnhardt Jr. Many of Hendrick's employees work at the company's 140-acre complex in Charlotte, North Carolina.[9]

When large racing teams like Hendrick travel to the speedway for a race, they send a smaller group of about thirty people to help in the pit.[10] The traveling team includes a driver, over-the-wall guys, a crew chief, and a spotter. The driver is the individual with the biggest influence in winning the race, but he needs a team.

The crew chief stays in touch with the driver and makes decisions about how to use personnel and resources to best help him or her. Some racing teams also have a car chief who assists the crew chief.

Pit stops are a necessary part of every race. They enable the team to refuel, change tires, clean the windshield, make minor repairs, or provide a drink for the driver. During a pit stop, seven over-the-wall guys climb the barrier and dash to the driver's aid.

A spotter watches the race from the top of the grandstands or from an upper level media area. The spotter provides a second set of eyes for the driver. The spotter scans for accidents ahead of the driver, debris on the road, and a safe opportunity to pass, then relays this information to the driver.

Greg Biffle distinguished himself as one of only a handful of drivers who has won races in each of NASCAR's top-three series.[11] Biffle states, "It's definitely a team sport, and we can't do what we do at all without a huge amount of effort."[12]

—•—

The apostles had a great pit crew ready to leap over the wall in an emergency and risk their lives for their leaders. Shocked by the news of James's death, Peter offered to help John, James's brother, retrieve the body from the authorities. Wasn't it enough that Herod had arrested Christians on trumped-up charges and beat them without cause? Now the persecution had escalated to murder, with the indignity of being beheaded with a sword instead of an ax.

Most executions were carried out with a sharpened ax. The thought of James's neck being hacked over and over again by a dull sword must have made Peter ill. He must have wondered if this was another attempt by Herod to gain popularity with the people.

How should the church respond to such treachery? James and John were among the founders of the early church. Their boldness ignited many in Jerusalem to speak courageously about Jesus. Were other church leaders in danger of being harassed or executed?

Peter, another founding apostle, encouraged the group to pray about how they could counter such evil with good. Passover was coming, and he wanted them to focus on the resurrection of Jesus, not the schemes of Herod.

Many Jewish visitors traveled to Jerusalem for the Passover. Christians stayed at home and celebrated with their families and other believers. At that time of year, life slowed down. They rejoiced and remembered the death, burial, and resurrection of their Savior.

Peter heard a knock on the door and opened for friends, but he was seized by Roman guards and taken to jail. Herod ordered the public trial (that is, execution) to be held on Monday, because it wasn't kosher to hold a "kangaroo court" during the feast. Those who belonged to the Jerusalem church prayed in earnest for Peter's release.

The night prior to his court date, Peter slept soundly with the help of saintly prayers. Someone nudged him in the middle of the night. When he realized the two guards chained to him were still asleep, he assumed it must have been one of the two soldiers who watched the door to his cell.

"Hurry! Get up."

Peter did not recognize the voice, but he obeyed. The handcuffs fell off of his wrists, and the individual barked more orders.

"Get dressed. Put on your shoes. Grab your coat and follow me."

A beam of light from the sky directed their path. They walked together past the first guard's post, then the second. When Peter and the stranger approached an iron gate that led to the city, it swung open on its own. As both continued on a familiar street, Peter saw his helper vanish right before his eyes. Peter then realized God had sent an angel to rescue him. He hurried to the home of Mary, the mother of John Mark, to seek sanctuary.

When Peter knocked, a young servant girl named Rhoda answered. Ecstatic to see him, she left him standing outside and ran to tell the others. The house was packed with late-night prayer warriors. They were so intent on interceding for Peter they did not believe Rhoda and continued their prayers.

But Peter persisted in knocking. When they finally opened the door, they were overwhelmed with joy.

Once Peter gained their attention, he related the saga of his escape. His friends chuckled at the thought of the uproar that would occur at the prison when the guards woke to find Peter gone. After the believers rejoiced together, Peter felt he should leave and lay low for a while. He feared if he remained it might endanger his friends.

This story from Acts 12:1–18 demonstrates what happens when members of a church pray for their beloved pastor. The church saw God answer in a mighty way.

Thomas Watson, a Puritan preacher who recognized the value of prayer in this passage, stated, "Who fetched the angel? The angel fetched Peter out of prison, but it was prayer that fetched the angel."[13] When we pray for our pastors, we tangibly assist them in ministry. We become part of the team.

Requirements of a Pit Crew Member

Many potential dangers threaten the pastorate. We must take on part of the burden our pastors carry by praying for them. Then they can continue to focus on preaching, teaching, and caring for their congregations. But how do we qualify to get into the race with our pastor? What is our role as a member of the pit crew? We are responsible for six things.

1. Love for Our Pastor

Heartfelt love for our pastors, their family, and their ministry tops the list of qualifications for a pit crew member. My nephew Chad is crazy about NASCAR. He watches races on TV, collects cards and other memorabilia, and shines his car until you can see your reflection. At one point he even built his own stock car and raced at local tracks. He doesn't worry about the time or money spent because he loves racing and everything that goes with it.

A passion for our pastors and the church will translate into generously giving our time and energy to pray for our leaders. Intercessors are loyal to their pastors and their churches. They commit themselves to intercede with purpose and conviction.

2. Living a Godly Life

Crew members strive to live a godly life. James 5:16 tells us, "The prayer of a righteous person is powerful and effective."

We want results for our petitions, so it is imperative to learn the ways of holy living.

We begin with knowing God's Word, which will teach us how to live and how to pray God's will.

We can be assured if we pray Scripture we are praying the will of God. First John 5:14 says, "This is the confidence we have in approaching God: that if we ask anything according to his will, he hears us."

In Andrew Murray's classic *With Christ in the School of Prayer*, he reminds us that prayer is not a monologue but a dialogue. Prayer is speaking to the Father, and when we read and meditate on the Word he speaks to us.[14]

Jesus teaches in John 15:7, "If you remain in me and my words remain in you, ask whatever you wish, and it will be done for you." This process drives us to go deeper and wait to see how God moves.

Tool Box

Pit stops on television look so easy. Yet crews rehearse as much as an hour a day in the garage before race day. A pit crew coach times and videotapes the practice sessions so he can analyze the tape to improve the team's technique. Racing garages install gym equipment so the seven crew members can lift weights and run. This enables each member to lift heavy tires and gas cans, and scamper around the car quickly during a pit stop.[15]

Prayer: Pray that you and other members of the pit crew will prepare yourselves adequately for the work of intercession.

Scripture: "Do your best to present yourself to God as one approved, a worker who does not need to be ashamed and who correctly handles the word of truth" *(2 Timothy 2:15).*

3. Submission to Authority

As quality crew members, we submit ourselves to authority. We desire to be accountable and to strive for righteousness. Those without a right attitude toward leadership predictably become frustrated and quit.

4. Humility

Intercessors do not seek recognition. The typical prayer warrior prefers to stay behind the scenes. Rather than looking for greater access to our pastors so they can serve us, we want to serve them.

5. Confidentiality

To keep confidences is a vital requirement for pit crew members. If we do not have the trust of our leadership, our pastor will not feel comfortable in sharing confidential information with us. These issues desperately demand our prayers. The number of pastors severely injured by gossip is shocking.

6. Availability.

Crew members need to be available. We must take inventory of our time to be sure we are not overcommitted. If we discover our calendar is too busy, we must drop to our knees and ask God to show us his priorities. Hectic schedules do not allow time for prayer.

Common Questions

Some will wonder, "Can I be in the pit crew if I do not have the spiritual gift of intercession?" Yes. God loves to hear us pray. First Thessalonians 5:17 urges us to "Pray continually." Just as everyone can evangelize, so everyone can pray.

The command in Matthew 28:19 to "Go and make disciples of all nations, baptizing them in the name of the Father and of the Son and of the Holy Spirit" is given to everyone. We are to evangelize even though we may not have the gift of evangelism. In the same way, we can all pray even if we do not have the gift of intercession.

A new believer may query, "Can I be a pastoral intercessor too?" Yes. You will require a teachable spirit. This goes back to humility, a critical ingredient in being an effective team member. We all need to continually deepen our prayer lives.

If you are new to the faith, read Bill Hybels's book *Too Busy Not to Pray*. If you are an experienced intercessor, consider reading or re-reading the classic *With Christ in the School of Prayer* by Andrew Murray.

Remember you do not have to be a pastor or a pastor's spouse to have an effective prayer ministry. I am, as many of you, just an ordinary person in the pew who has a passion to pray for my pastor and to recruit others to join me.

Role of a Pit Crew Member

The bottom line of our commitment as pit crew members is to *pray daily*. Ask the Holy Spirit to lead you to pray for what your pastor needs. Pray the promptings of the Spirit rather than trying to make a fix-it list for your shepherd. Our pastors do not need our advice or our counsel. They need our prayers.

"I looked for someone among them who would build up the wall and stand before me in the gap on behalf of the land so I would not have to destroy it, but I found no one" (Ezekiel 22:30).

God searches for individuals who will build a wall of prayer around our shepherds to protect them from harm and sin.

Bob Roberts, senior pastor of Northwood Church in Fort Worth, Texas, said, "We pastors need prayer covering from our church members. There doesn't have to be a huge 'intercession ministry' to do this. It only takes two or three people who will agree to pray for their leadership. They should be people of spiritual depth and maturity, people who see prayers answered and who can keep confidences."[16]

Once again, we must be trustworthy. Even an unintentional leak of a confidential request can be devastating to our pastors. They will feel betrayed. Also, we must be patient when our pastors do not share needs with us. They may not feel comfortable yet with how much they can trust us.

Don't expect praise or recognition for your time and efforts. Neither should we assume that our pastors' gratitude will include praying for us. This is a sacrifice of love.

Race Plan

The goal of any race is to win. As in many other sports, the best strategy for winning in NASCAR is to promote teamwork. Let's identify who comprises the race team and see how that team compares to our pastoral prayer team.

Pit to Pulpit

The Southern Baptist Convention reported that 969 pastors were terminated in 2005. The general inability to "get along" was cited as the root cause for the majority of the firings or resignations under pressure.[17]

Prayer: Pray for your pastor and congregation to work together as a team.

Scripture: "Hatred stirs up conflict, but love covers over all wrongs" *(Proverbs 10:12).*

Fans at the racetrack are similar to a congregation. Brad Keselowski fans are enthusiastic about getting to know Keselowski better. They want to know everything about him. They collect memorabilia, read about him in books and on the internet. When they go to a race, they watch his every move and try to get his autograph.

In a similar way, members of a church learn about their pastors so they will know how to pray for them. I don't mean that church members should be as fanatical as some sports fans. Please don't stop your minister on his way to the pulpit and ask for an autograph in your Bible!

Yet we should learn about our pastors' salvation stories and their calls to ministry. Find out what desires God has placed on their hearts. Think of their strengths and pray for God to use them in a mighty way. If they mention something that causes them to struggle, then write it down as a prayer request. Learn about their family's needs. Find out what they like to do to relax.

If all the people in the pew knows this basic information about the pastor, we will be knowledgeable enough to pray. This minimal commitment enables us to cheer the pastor to the finish line through intercession.

The race team can be likened to the prayer team in our local church. These individuals minister to our church and pastor through intercession. This group exists as a subset of the congregation. Group members dedicate their time to pray for the pastor. The team keeps informed of the prayer needs through consistent meetings and communications.

The traveling team resembles the pit crew. This group specializes in praying for the pastor. The crew may pray as a group for the pastor as he steps into the pulpit, or it may assign individuals to pray throughout the sermon.

The team leader communicates with the preacher about their prayer needs, organizes prayer times, and prepares prayer guides. As your team grows, your pit crew leader may need an assistant.

A pit crew leader may consider choosing a small group of prayer warriors (over-the-wall guys) to be ready at a moment's notice to pray for the pastor -- to refresh and renew him or her for the next set of laps. The team will need spiritual warfare intercessors, who function as spotters, to keep the pastor from the dangers brought by our enemy,

Satan plans to wreck the pastor's ministry. If each member of the pit crew understands the race strategy and faithfully prays, everyone will celebrate the finish.

3

Personal Walk with God

Driver Preparation

WINNING WISDOM

Real prayer comes not from gritting our teeth,
but from falling in love.

RICHARD FOSTER

In NASCAR, every fan knows it takes a good driver to win a race. During his career, Richard Petty, known as The King of stock-car racing, acquired seven championships and over two hundred wins. His success earned him spots in the Motorsports Hall of Fame of America in 1989, the International Motorsports Hall of Fame in 1997, and the NASCAR Hall of Fame in 2010. Petty raced for thirty-five years and remains a stock-car icon because of his record number of wins and adoration by NASCAR fans.[18]

Some people assume drivers simply hop in a car and cruise around in circles on Sunday afternoons. Not so. Being competitive requires physical strength and stamina. Temperatures can rise to 120 degrees inside the vehicle. Each driver sports a heavy, fire-retardant jumpsuit plus a helmet. At speeds ranging from 180 to over 200 miles per hour, the driver must employ quick reaction times and extreme focus. Many drivers work out on a consistent basis to increase their endurance, stay sharp throughout the race, and develop the strength to wrestle a car that may not be handling well.[19]

Like winning NASCAR drivers, pastors need preparation to be successful. Our pastors may be gifted in preaching and teaching, but if their own personal walk with God is not in order, they cannot be the mighty leader God has called them to be. And pastors must lead by example. If their personal lives deteriorate into disarray, their speech and behavior will send conflicting messages about the Christian life.

When pastors were surveyed as to their number-one priority, 86 percent said it was their personal relationship with God.[20]

Elated by this statistic, I became puzzled when I read that a survey of 572 pastors conducted by Peter Wagner revealed the average pastor spends just 22 minutes a day in prayer. Wagner also found 57 percent spend less than 20 minutes a day in prayer.[21] What keeps them from their stated goal?

Craig Groeschel, in his book *Confessions of a Pastor,* writes this admission: "As I approached the pulpit, the truth hit me squarely between the eyes. I hadn't prayed at all. Not that day. Not the day before. Not the day before that. To the best of my knowledge, I hadn't prayed all week."[22]

Groeschel explained that after he stumbled through the sermon, he spent the following week in prayer. He agonized over how to face his then two-hundred-member congregation. In the next sermon, he confessed to his flock what he had already admitted to God. He knelt at the altar that week with a lot of company because pastors and parishioners face the same hang-ups in having a consistent devotional time with God. Working through their struggle together proved fruitful.

From that point in 1996, LifeChurch.tv has become a multi-campus church with numerous worship experiences in fifteen locations and online.

Tool Box

In the drivers' compound at a raceway, it is not unusual to see NASCAR drivers start a friendly competition with their remote-controlled cars. Fellow drivers report that Tony Stewart competes to the point where he burns the rubber off his tires during these mini-races. It seems these drivers cannot get enough.[23]

Prayer: Pray that your pastor will continually yearn to know God.

Scripture: "As the deer pants for streams of water, so my soul pants for you, my God. My soul thirsts for God, for the living God. When can I go and meet with God?" *(Psalm 42:1–2).*

Road Blocks

Terry Muck, past editor of *Leadership Journal*, sent a survey to 500 readers about their devotional lives. When asked what their hindrances were, 34 percent indicated time, 9 percent listed distractions, 7 percent said consistency, and 6 percent answered discipline.[24]

When the issue of a consistent quiet time comes up in my Bible studies and small groups, these same issues are mentioned. In every discussion, time emerges as the biggest culprit.

This is not a new problem. In 1948, before most of us were born, A. W. Tozer wrote the following in his book, *The Pursuit of God.* "We Christians must simplify our lives or lose untold treasures on earth and in eternity. Modern civilization is so complex as to make the devotional life all but impossible. The need for solitude and quietness was never greater than it is today."[25]

Tozer died in 1963, long before the tech revolution, personal computers, smart phones, and social media became everyday life.[26] I find no evidence that the pace of our society will slow down, so Tozer's statement remains critical.

None of us were born reading our Bibles, praying, worshiping, journaling, or meditating. Somewhere in our spiritual development, each of us received the gift of salvation and became a new creature in Christ.

Second Corinthians 5:17 describes this gift. "Therefore, if anyone is in Christ, the new creation has come: the old has gone, the new is here!"

At some point we became curious about the changes in our lives. We began a new relationship, and we wanted to know more about our Savior. Meeting with our Lord each day enables us to know him more intimately. We must alter our routines to form this daily habit of meeting with God.

Root Issues and Remedies

Psychologists tell us four issues lie at the root of any lifestyle change. Underlying the transformation, we weigh—many times subconsciously—these factors as we either avoid or embrace a practice. An accurate diagnosis will help us cure our inconsistency.[27] Let's ask ourselves these four questions:

1. Does it work for me?

When my family relocated to the Kansas City area, we attended a church in Shawnee, Kansas. A godly young mother in that community struggled several years with cancer. The congregation rallied to pray earnestly for her healing. After her death, reactions of church members ranged from anger at God to disillusionment about God's mercy. As I talked with them, many shared the expectation their dear friend would be miraculously healed. They resolved to give up on prayer because it had not worked.

The remedy for that disappointment involved helping them see the various aspects of prayer. They had focused on intercession. Over the months that followed, intercessors looked inward to see why their prayers received no response. One businessman testified he prayed with wrong motives. A school teacher said her relationship with God deepened. An elder expressed how his prayer life reached another level. Over time, these faithful prayer warriors realized God answered prayer in a far greater way than they ever dreamed.

2. Am I able to do it?

After a chapel service in the Christian school where I worked, a distressed junior high student came to my office. Amy said she did not enjoy a daily QT (quiet time with God). She worked hard to make average grades, but she read below grade level and did not like to read. Amy believed reading the Bible everyday would help her grow spiritually, but she had convinced herself she could not do it.

Christians such as Amy need a boost of confidence through verbal encouragement. To build their morale, they need someone to help them with small experiences of success. By joining a discipleship group, they will benefit from the encouragement of others in their quest to be faithful.

Amy joined a D-group (discipleship group) sponsored by her youth group. The gals in her group recommended that she listen to the Bible in an audio format. They also inspired Amy to be consistent with her quiet time.

3. Is it worth it to me?

Darren turned to Christianity many years ago. He actively serves in his church as an adult Bible study teacher. His children have left the nest, and he looks forward to having grandchildren. The pressures of family life he once experienced seem a distant memory, and he does not see the need to deepen his relationship with God. His life appears to be okay. Why try to make it better through prayer and Bible study?

Pit to Pulpit

Thom Rainer, president and CEO of LifeWay Christian Resources, wrote about losing a dear prayer warrior who had lifted him up for sixteen years. At age ninety, Nell Bruce finished her work as an intercessor and passed on to heaven. Rainer said, "I know that my life and ministry were incredibly blessed and protected because she spoke to the Father on my behalf."[28]

Prayer: Pray for more crew members like Nell Bruce to pray for your pastor.

Scripture: "Brothers and sisters, pray for us" *(1 Thessalonians 5:25).*

This factor is the most subtle and difficult to diagnose. We assume any Christian will value the outcome of spiritual disciplines. However, Darren had developed a comfortable condition. He requires help to see the value in a devotional life. Darren needs to consider whether peace with God, more intimacy, increased confidence, integrity, and insight into God's mysteries deserve his time and effort.

A follower of Jesus who remains satisfied with his or her current state needs spiritual renewal to revive spiritual thirst.

4. What will it cost?

My husband and I fostered several children in our home. One of these, a teenager named Emily, became a Christian. At the promptings of her youth pastor, she began a devotional time. She decided to get up fifteen minutes earlier each morning, which required an earlier bed time. On the nights we watched a ballgame or the news, Emily trotted off to bed. It was easy to pass up these shows because they didn't interest her. But the evening her favorite sitcom came on, she stood with one foot in the living room and one foot in the hallway leading to her room. She asked for our help.

Our goal was to help Emily count the cost. We helped her to see the worth of time alone with God. As she did, she became willing to pay a higher price. Not only did she develop consistency, but the time she spent reading and praying grew longer.

In the case of a new believer, keep the cost low. A five-minute-a-day quiet time works better than an overwhelming hour-long attempt.

Reaction

When I considered my quiet time in light of the four diagnostic questions, I paused at "Is it worth it to me?" Although I practice a daily time that includes Bible reading, prayer, meditation, journaling, and memorization, it disturbs me when I don't thirst to dig still deeper.

When my pastor sees me, does he notice someone with a vitality and freshness about her walk with God? Does my countenance challenge him to hunger for more of God? I do not want my faith walk to level off. My own research caused me to shake up my devotional time and change how I do my daily time with God.

Our pastors can fall into the same kind of ruts. Our role is not to diagnose or recommend treatment for our pastors. That falls to the Holy Spirit. Our responsibility rests on self-examination, using the previous four questions. By doing so, we make needed repairs and maintain a consistent devotional time, which includes prayer for our pastor.

Requests

Prayers for our pastors should be preventive prayers. Address the four roadblocks to consistent devotional time. Pray that our pastors' expectations of their daily time persists and results in intimacy with the Savior. Ask God to give them boldness and confidence as they pray and study. Pray they will be continually renewed by the value of knowing Jesus. Ask God to help them count the cost and realize the incalculable worth of a more vital relationship with their Lord.

As God answers our petitions, the entire congregation will notice our pastor's high-octane spiritual life, revved up to serve God.

4

Pastoral Roles

The Driver on Race Day

WINNING WISDOM

*Church members have much more to do than go to church as
curious, idle spectators to be amused and entertained. It is their
business to pray mightily that the Holy Ghost will clothe the
preacher with power and make his words like dynamite.*

CHERYL SACKS

Fans go to a NASCAR Sprint Cup race with certain expectations.
Before the race, some tailgate in the parking lot. A sizeable
number make their way to the infield to obtain an autograph
from their favorite driver. Others head straight for the memorabilia
shops or refreshment stands.

After they make it to their seats, fans hope for no injuries but look
forward to an exciting race with many lead changes. They assume the

competition will include some door smacking, bumper banging, and swapping of paint. Fans anticipate calamities such as blown engines, burning tires, yellow-flag accidents. Most of all, they look forward to a dramatic finish.

But on July 9, 2011, the rural roadways could not handle the traffic volume of 107,000 fans at the newly opened Kentucky Speedway. When the race started, fans sat stranded in a ten-mile traffic quagmire stretching in both directions. About 1,500 ticketholders could not get to the Kentucky Speedway for the inaugural Sprint Cup Series (now called the Monster Energy NASCAR Cup Series). These disappointed fans heard via radio that Kyle Busch crossed the finish line.[29]

Most of us, even children, have some sense of how things should work. Take the story of Vivian, for instance. She put on her pink dotted Swiss blouse for the first day of school. She picked up her backpack, marked with her name and filled with school supplies. Vivian slung it over her lacy-white overlay, which she tucked underneath the inch-wide straps. She grabbed her Cinderella lunchbox from the kitchen and hugged her mom as she left the front door. My friend, Mary, waved as her daughter strolled to the curb with her head high. Vivian marched up the bus steps and the yellow doors closed behind her.

Later that sunny afternoon, Mary waited on the porch for the bus to return. The giggling and talking of children drowned out the sound of the bus engine. Mom heard a couple of goodbyes as her child appeared.

With a scowl on her face, Vivian stomped down the bus steps. She then stuffed her lunchbox into her backpack and dragged it down the sidewalk. As she trudged to the porch, she jerked on the lace at her hemline. With her hands on her hips, she halted.

"It was awful!"

Mary put her arm around her daughter and squeezed lightly. "What happened, Vivian?"

Vivian explained how the teacher asked each child to tell her name and what her dad did for a living. Boys and girls proudly answered that their dads were policemen, carpenters, bankers, and truck drivers. When it was Vivian's turn, she hung her head.

"My dad doesn't do anything," she said. "He's just a preacher."

Even though we chuckle at this kindergartener's response, it is not a laughing matter. Many in our congregations are equally confused about the role of the pastor. Some church members think ministers work only one day a week and have no clue how complicated it is to lead a church.

The work of the church is to redeem and rebuild lives, which is a complicated and intangible process that can be difficult to explain. The workforce for this endeavor usually consists completely of volunteers, who may come and go as they please. Recruiting can be difficult because serving includes no pay and requires hours away from family. Also most pastors will suffer on the road to maturity.

Bill Hybels has mentioned that the church is the most leadership-intensive enterprise in society. He feels it remains far more difficult to lead a church than to operate a business. Hybels knows because he has done both.[30]

Super-Sized Super Hero?

NASCAR drivers do far more than drive in circles on Sunday afternoons. Most are family men who bring their wives and kids with them to the track. Drivers are role models to kids and are expected to act accordingly. Due to the many contracts they sign with sponsors and licensing agreements for NASCAR merchandise, drivers must be shrewd businessmen.

They also must be public relations experts as they make appearances for sponsors, field questions from reporters, and sign autographs for fans. In 1998, the cooling system that shot air into

Ricky Rudd's helmet and through his seat failed during a race at Martinsville Speedway. He managed to finish the race in first place even though temperatures inside the car reached 150 degrees.

Rudd, covered with blisters and burns on his backside, required help to get out of his car in Victory Lane. While paramedics gave him oxygen, Rudd lay on the ground. He was barely able to talk as he gave post-race interviews.[31]

People in the pews expect valiant acts from their clergy as well. Pollster George Barna found in 2001 that churchgoers insist their pastors juggle an average of sixteen major tasks.[32] Each member has his own idea of what the minister does. Most assume their cleric will be a dynamic preacher and teacher, terrific administrator, savvy politician, understanding counselor, expert in conflict resolution, perfect spouse, and wonderful parent. How can our pastors minister with such expectations placed on them?

In his first year as a solo pastor in a small church, Trevor Lee, who now serves as pastor of Mountair Christian Church in Lakewood, Colorado, learned this truth: "People had things they believed they needed and expectations of what the pastor was supposed to provide."

Many of the requests were not a big deal so he complied. However, Lee said, "In other cases, I responded to expectations by helping them see they weren't really needs."

Pastor Lee, overwhelmed on Sunday mornings with announcements, communion, prayer time, singing, transitions, and sermon, found members also expected him to do a children's sermon. He did so for a few weeks while he urged individuals to use their gifts and offered them the opportunity. He realized that to ignore people's expectations would be perceived as failure.[33]

Beyond parishioners' expectations, pastors have their own thoughts of what the ideal pastor should be. "In the first church I served, everyone talked about 'breaking the 200 barrier,'" said Jack

Connell, professor of pastoral ministry at Northeastern Seminary at Roberts Wesleyan College. But when attendance passed two hundred, Connell found himself in competition with his friends who led churches of 300 to 400.[34]

Setting goals to win more people to Christ can be a valid expectation. But pray that your pastor's motivation to grow will be based on love for people, not ego or a desire to win.

Pit to Pulpit

A 2017 Barna study indicated 29 percent of ministers felt unprepared to counsel, 29 percent had difficulty handling administration, and 27 percent expressed that they were ill-equipped to handle conflict.[35]

Prayer: Pray that our leaders will not worry about their inadequacies but will rely on the adequacy of God.

Scripture: "Not that we are competent in ourselves to claim anything for ourselves, but our competence comes from God" *(2 Corinthians 3:5).*

Some pastors feel overwhelmed as they strive to be the model minister. They may concoct an image and seek to emulate it. But while our pastors try to "look good under the hood," their personal lives and families may be weak and thin, like cheap motor oil. We must pray that our pastors will desire to be what God wants them to be.

Pastors are fallible human beings who may be lonely, stressed, and discouraged. The pastor exerts the greatest influence on the spiritual development of the church. Our pastors need our support and encouragement to be effective. Most of all, they need our prayers.

Seven Days of Service

With all the confusion about their roles, how do we know what to pray for our pastors? The Word of God categorizes the responsibilities of the clergy into seven areas. Since there are seven days in the week, we can pray for one of these responsibilities each day.

Sunday

Pray for our pastors as preacher-teachers, that they will understand and communicate God's truth. Most churchgoers surveyed by Barna put this on their list of expectations for their pastors.

Paul does too. He writes in Ephesians 6:19, "Pray also for me, that whenever I speak, words may be given me so that I will fearlessly make known the mystery of the gospel."

Robin Sigars, lead pastor at Carterville Christian Church in Missouri, wrote that he would like his parishioners to pray for "Wisdom in the word! Fire in my heart to preach! That God would lay upon my heart the words he knows our church needs to hear to change their lives."[36]

This advice from John Ortberg to young preachers can also guide our prayers. "Guard your study time. Be ruthless about studying, preparing, and feeding your mind. Learn how you receive input best, whether from people or reading or solitude. Know what feeds you. Spiritually speaking, the more you teach, the more you need solitude and to hear God."[37]

Monday

Pray for your pastor's personal walk with the Lord. Just like you and me, pastors' ministries will never advance past their faithfulness in Bible study and prayer (see 2 Timothy 2:15 and Philippians 4:6–7). A lack of time in Scripture leaves ministers without direction, and their prayers become powerless. Like the priests in the Old Testament, our pastors need to pray a covering of protection over their congregation.

Ministers are called to be persons of integrity and committed to personal purity, without a trace of immorality. Without these qualities, pastors might succeed when measured by worldly standards but fail by God's standard (see Ephesians 5:3–5, Psalm 51:10). There are no shortcuts to holiness.

Peter Scazzero, author of *The Emotionally Healthy Church*, wrote, "It is an illusion to imagine that we can lead our people on a spiritual journey we have not taken. No program can substitute for the superficiality and self-will that inevitably permeate our ministry when we skim in our relationship with God."[38]

Tuesday

Focus on the role of pastoral caregiver. Caring for the flock can be a draining responsibility. The number of people in our congregations who are hurting and desperately need comfort and compassion is staggering. Ezekiel 34:1–6 contains harsh words for shepherds who do not nurture and protect their flocks.

During a board meeting on strategic planning, a board member turned to his minister and blurted, "But we don't need a CEO. We need a pastor!" At the time, this pastor passed off the comment as well-intended but naïve about the complexities of ministry. Nearly twenty years later, this leader admitted he had been enamored with the latest leadership and business best practices. He lost "sight of the heart and soul of pastoral ministry."[39]

Pray that your pastors will know their sheep, be good listeners, be full of compassion, and genuinely care for their flocks (see John 10:14).

Wednesday

Pray for pastors as they fulfill the role of prophet. As prophets, our pastors need a spiritual GPS to search for God's will. They need to be tuned into God's truth for today's world.

Pray from 2 Timothy 4:2, "Preach the Word; be prepared in season and out of season; correct, rebuke and encourage—with great patience and careful instruction."

Pray for pastors to possess wisdom and compassion when they deal with people who need to be convinced, reprimanded, or exhorted.

This may be the toughest responsibility any pastor encounters. I recall a cartoon posted on a church-office bulletin board in which a preacher remarks to his spouse, "I told them the truth, and they set me free."

Pete Scazzero serves as pastor of New Life Fellowship Church in Queens, New York. He says, "It is easy to engage in false peace by appeasing people. It's hard to speak truth when they may become angry."[40]

Confrontation is not for the fainthearted. Pray Joshua 1:9, "Do not be afraid; do not be discouraged, for the Lord your God will be with you wherever you go."

Robin Sigars explains the toughest thing for him as a pastor: "To have to sit down and confront a person in my church with the sin of his life and how that sin is destroying him (physically and spiritually). How sin is destroying the family."[41]

Thursday

Pray for the minister as pastoral leader. In their book *Leaders: Strategies for Taking Charge*, Warren Bennis and Burt Nanus sited over 850 definitions of leadership.[42]

Henry and Richard Blackaby provide a simple definition: "Spiritual leadership is moving people on to God's agenda."[43]

Our pastors equip and mentor new believers and leaders (see 2 Timothy 2:2). Leaders need to motivate staff as well as congregation members, so pray Proverbs 27:17, "As iron sharpens iron, so one person sharpens another."

When mistakes occur, a spiritual leader accepts responsibility, acts with transparency, and apologizes (see Psalm 139:23–24).

Persistence rates as a key component, so pray Romans 12:8: "If it is to lead, do it diligently."

Wise decisions are crucial. Before God led him to enter politics and run for governor of Arkansas, Mike Huckabee led a 2,500-member church in Arkadelphia. Huckabee commented, "I faced situations every day that were insurmountable without using the faith God had given me to make decisions."[44]

Friday

Be in prayer for our pastors' evangelism and prayer efforts. Pray they will communicate the good news with such enthusiasm, members will join the effort to reach those who desperately need Christ.

Pray Acts 1:8: "But you will receive power when the Holy Spirit comes on you; and you will be my witnesses in Jerusalem, and in all Judea and Samaria, and to the ends of the earth."

Pastors need to convey to their congregations the importance of praying for the lost. Intercede with Romans 10:1: "Brothers, my heart's desire and prayer to God . . . is that they may be saved."

Some church leaders may incur opposition when they urge the laity to shift gears from an internally focused ministry to an external approach.

Rick Rusaw, author of *The Externally Focused Church*, experienced resistance from staff and members when he cancelled an annual Christmas production with an attendance of 30,000. Instead, he transferred the resources and manpower of the massive attraction into activities that put his church members into the community. Rusaw felt his church needed to grow in both numbers and depth, but LifeBridge Christian Church's programming had been conducted primarily inside the church walls.

He wrote, "The best church leaders manage the tension between maintenance and development. It's like the tension between tire and pavement. Too little and you'll wreck; too much and you won't get anywhere. If a pastor is more maintenance-oriented, he or she is not likely to be in a growing church."[45]

Pray that our church leaders will maintain a balanced approach.

Saturday

Pray for our pastors' families. Given the heavy demands of ministry, many clergy struggle to find time for family. In a *Leadership Journal* survey, 25 percent of pastors' spouses responded that their husband's busy work schedule created conflict in the home.[46]

Bob Schmidgall, pastor at Calvary Church in Naperville, Illinois, admitted, "I haven't been a perfect father. Some weeks I don't take my day off, and I'm not proud of that." After this confession in *Good Pastor, Good Parent*, Schmidgall reworked his calendar and made family time paramount.[47]

Pray 1 Timothy 3:5 for our ministers. "If anyone does not know how to manage his own family, how can he take care of God's church?"

"If you are married, your vocation is your spouse first, and any children God has given you. This covenant takes priority over our church and people," wrote Pete Scazzero.[48]

Pray that our pastors' marriages will endure and that they nurture a good relationship with each of their children.

A Symbol of Support

Toolbox

In the world of racing, a driver and a racer are two different people. A driver drives race cars, while a racer knows how to drive a race car as well as build his car from the ground up. Drivers and racers both win races, but to be referred to as a racer rates as the ultimate compliment.[49]

Prayer: Thank God for the ministry of our pastors and for the opportunity to intercede for them.

Scripture: "I have not stopped giving thanks for you, remembering you in my prayers" *(Ephesians 1:16).*

To pray these seven requests involves only a few minutes each day, but the dividends it pays boggle the mind. When an opportunity occurs, tell your pastor you will pray each day. Be prepared for your minister to become overwhelmed with emotion.

You may want to present your pastor with a gift as a reminder of your daily intercession. In her book *Caring for Your Pastor*, Lorna Dobson relates the story of a couple who gave her and her husband, Ed, a statue of Moses with his hands upheld by Aaron and Hur.

In Exodus 17:8–15 we read how Moses sent Joshua to lead the Israelites into battle against the Amalekites. At the same time, Moses journeyed to the top of the hill at Rephidim and held up the staff of God. When Moses grew tired and lowered his hands, the battle turned, and the Israelites began to lose. So Aaron and Hur stepped up and hoisted Moses upon a rock. Then, with one on each side, Aaron and Hur upheld Moses' hands, leading to an Israelite victory. For the Dobsons, this sculpture became a symbol of their prayer support.[50]

You may want to give your pastor a copy of this book with a note of encouragement included on the front page. Or perhaps you could purchase a Matchbox or Hot Wheels die-cast race car and include a note explaining how you are interceding for them to finish the race. Keep up your support. Keep your hands and heart lifted in prayer for your pastor.

5

Protection

Race Safety

WINNING WISDOM

The Devil is not terribly frightened of our human efforts and credentials. But he knows his kingdom will be damaged when we begin to lift up our hearts to God.

Jim Cymbala

Damon sat up in bed and grabbed his laptop. He clicked to retrieve his email as he rubbed the sleep out of his eyes. Why did it take so long to come up? Three emails appeared simultaneously, but none of the messages was the one he wanted. Damon slammed his computer shut and fell back in bed. His boss Luke promised to let him know by eight o'clock whether the board had approved the strategic plan. What caused the hold up?

Damon concluded that fretting would accomplish nothing, so he should shower and get dressed. Besides, once the email did post, it could contain action items to be implemented immediately. Invigorated by the meetings of the past two days, he sang in the steamy shower. "We shall overcome." Damon turned off the water, slipped into his work clothes, and combed his hair. "We shall overcome." In front of the mirror, he straightened his tie and ran a comb through his hair a second time. "We shall overcome someday."

He fetched his laptop and got back online, but still no email from Luke. So he opened the file of the SWOT analysis he and his coworkers had worked through two days ago. His team brainstormed strengths, weaknesses, opportunities, and threats for a full day. As strengths of the organization, participants mentioned the great abilities of leadership, street-smart employees, a well-organized firm with a history of success, and a staff motivated to win.

Damon scrolled down to read his notes on weaknesses. He recalled the eeric silence when no one volunteered an answer. Luke Lyon, who founded the company and served as CEO, glared from person to person. Luke lit a cigarillo and asked, "Anyone mind if I smoke?" No one said a word.

The CEO glanced at his watch. "It's time for lunch," he said. "Everyone back in an hour." Luke stormed out, leaving a trail of smoke. Participants sat stunned for several minutes before they quietly filed out of the room.

The afternoon session rolled along peacefully. Employees hashed over opportunities for overtaking the competition, but one idea surfaced over and over again.

"Go after the leadership."

"If you take out the head, then the rest of the organization will be so damaged it can't recover," one staff member offered.

"Right," another chimed in. "Discredit the leader. That will do it."

The assessment of threats produced comments centered on two topics. First, staff members were concerned rivals might discover company plans and fashion a strategy to combat it. Some members of the group worried the competition might discover the true purpose of Lyon Enterprises. Remarks such as, "We don't want any more claims that our advertising is false or misleading," got Luke's attention.

"I directed the advertising department to air ads that express statements of fact," he responded. Luke crossed his arms and continued. "Now if something else happens, I can retain plausible deniability because I never viewed the commercials before they aired." As he leaned forward, he explained, "If we do receive complaints, I will fire a couple of ad executives and send them off with a fine severance package."

As Damon scrolled through the remainder of the SWOT assessment, a notice popped up to indicate a new email. It was a message from Luke with the strategic plan his group had worked on the previous day attached.

"Damon, the board unanimously agreed. We love the plan and we want you to spearhead the turnaround project. Our board chair added a couple of items he found successful in the past."

With a big smile on his face, Damon leaped up and danced around the room. *This is the moment I always dreamed about. The board finally noticed my brilliance and undying efforts.* After several minutes, he collapsed from exhaustion into a chair and opened the file to survey his assignment.

Strategic Five-Year Plan for Lyon Enterprises

Perilous Pastor Project
Board Chair: Lou C. Fur
Chief Executive Officer: Luke Lyon
Project Manager: Damon Demon

Mission Statement: The purpose of Lyon Enterprises continues to be to extinguish Christianity. This charge requires all churches be forced out of business so believers are isolated, defenseless, and under our control.

Situation: A survey of our current status indicates great losses. Rather than deteriorating, churches have strengthened, grown, and matured. Church growth remains our principal obstacle. All efforts and resources should be directed to reverse this trend.

Target: Because of the importance of leadership in a church, our primary strategy will focus on the pastor. Steps to this end include:

(1) Convince pastors of growing churches they alone are responsible for the success of the church.

(2) To decrease pastors' performance, increase stress in every possible situation.

(3) As pastors seek to find rest, introduce seductive and subtle distractions that will divert them onto destructive tangents away from their mission.

(4) Constantly accuse those who have engaged in inappropriate behavior and speech, and remind them of their shame.

(5) If little or no headway can be made with the pastors, then refocus attacks on the home, driving a wedge between pastors and their families.

Know Your Enemy

Lyon Enterprises does not exist, but this fictitious company does represent the mission and some of the strategies employed by the powers of darkness. The beginnings of this war for supremacy are described in Isaiah 14:12–15, where the five "I will" statements of Satan are recorded, proving his intention to make himself greater than God.

> "How you have fallen from heaven,
>   morning star, son of the dawn!
> You have been cast down to the earth,
>   you who once laid low the nations!
> You said in your heart,
>   "I will ascend to the heavens;
> I will raise my throne
>   above the stars of God;
> I will sit enthroned on the mount of assembly,
>   on the utmost heights of Mount Zaphon.
> I will ascend above the tops of the clouds;
>   I will make myself like the Most High."
> But you are brought down to the realm of the dead,
>   to the depths of the pit."

When dismissed from heaven (see 1 Timothy 3:6), Satan took a host of angelic beings with him to serve as his foot soldiers. As members of the family of God, we are their targets. As a leader of your church, your pastor is an especially high-value target.

During the Battle of Saratoga of the American Revolution, American commander Daniel Morgan ordered: "Forget the poor fellows who fight for sixpence a day. Concentrate your fire on the epaulet men!"

Epaulets were ornamental shoulder pieces used as insignia of rank by the armed forces. Morgan's tactic of aiming for the officers rather than the rank-and-file soldiers resulted in such a depletion of officers that British general John Burgoyne was forced to surrender. Many historians regard the Battle of Saratoga as the turning point of the American Revolution.[51]

Without prayer warriors like you and me to intercede, our churches could see their leadership knocked out of the race.

Today, many Christians in America don't believe Satan exists. In a 2008 survey of 1,871 adults, the Barna Group found 59 percent either strongly agreed or somewhat agreed that Satan "is not a living being but a symbol of evil."[52]

Rick Warren of Saddleback Church disagrees. He said, "If you don't take the Christian life seriously, if you don't take ministry seriously, the Devil's going to. You may not mean business, but he does."[53]

Pit to Pulpit

Watchman Nee, a Chinese author and pastor who was severely persecuted by the Communists, once said, "Satan has in fact a plan against the saints of the Most High which is to wear them out. Now, were Satan to strike the children of God with great force at one time, they would know exactly how to resist the enemy since they would immediately recognize his work. He uses the method of gradualism to wear down the people of God."[54] Apparently, our enemy's plan works, because 37 percent of pastors surveyed by Barna were judged to be at either high or medium risk of burnout.[55]

Prayer: Pray that your pastor will rest in Jesus.

Scripture: "Therefore, with minds that are alert and fully sober, set your hope on the grace to be brought to you when Jesus Christ is revealed at his coming" *(1 Peter 1:13)*.

In 2 Corinthians 2:11 and 11:3, the apostle Paul states that Satan possesses wit and craftiness.

In Luke 22:31, Jesus claims Satan desires to harm believers. The apostle John records that he fills with anger (Revelation 12:12).

Revelation 2:9 exposes our adversary's organizational skills, revealing that he has developed his own synagogue.

Pray for our pastors to acknowledge their adversary. As 1 Peter 5:8 warns, "Be alert and of sober mind. Your enemy the devil prowls around like a roaring lion looking for someone to devour."

The Enemy Tries to Deceive

The first attack against the human race occurred in the Garden of Eden. The Father of Lies employed his favorite strategy: deception. Scripture warns us about the three ways Satan uses deception: self-deception, false prophets and teachers, and deceiving spirits.

Self-deception

It is shocking to realize how many Bible verses mention the different ways we can deceive ourselves. The eight self-deceptions identified are subtle ways sin may creep into our lives.

When asked how the Evil One might like to damage him, Earl Palmer, pastor of First Presbyterian Church in Berkeley, California, explained: "I'm tempted to think that because things are going well or the budget is met or people are appreciating what I preach, I no longer need to be under discipline. Or that the doctrine of sin doesn't really apply to me because I've been given a special position. That's a common danger."[56] Scripture lists a number of ways in which we may deceive ourselves.

"Do not deceive yourselves. If any of you think
you are wise by the standards of this age, you should

become 'fools' so that you may become wise. For the wisdom of this world is foolishness in God's sight. As it is written: 'He catches the wise in their craftiness'" (1 Corinthians 3:18–19).

"Or do you not know that wrongdoers will not inherit the kingdom of God? Do not be deceived: Neither the sexually immoral nor idolaters nor adulterers nor men who have sex with me nor thieves nor the greedy nor drunkards nor slanderers nor swindlers will inherit the kingdom of God?" (1 Corinthians 6:9–10).

"Do not be deceived: 'Bad company corrupts good morals'" (1 Corinthians 15:33 NASB).

"If anyone thinks they are something when they are not, they deceive themselves" (Galatians 6:3).

"Do not be deceived: God cannot be mocked. A man reaps what he sows" (Galatians 6:7).

Do not merely listen to the word, and so deceive yourselves. Do what it says" (James 1:22).

"Those who consider themselves religious and yet do not keep a tight rein on their tongues deceive themselves, and their religion is worthless" (James 1:26).

"If we claim to be without sin, we deceive ourselves and the truth is not in us" (1 John 1:8).

Harold Bussell, former dean of the chapel at Gordon College and preaching pastor of First Congregational Church in Hamilton, Massachusetts, expresses the remedy to self-deception, "True discernment comes from self-examination. Refusing to deal with our own potential for evil makes even our goodness dangerous."[57] Will you pray for your pastor to recognize and guard against these self-deceptions?

False Prophets and Teachers

When we mention false prophets and teachers, many of us think of cult leaders such as David Koresh, a high school dropout and polygamist,[58] or Jim Jones, described by childhood acquaintances as "really weird" and obsessed with religion and death.[59] We surmise they prey on the young, the mentally ill, or seniors who suffer from dementia.

More often, these dangerous counterfeits appear to be studied religious leaders who prey upon everyday people who seek a deeper experience with God.

Many believers laughed about Harold Camping's prediction the world would end on May 21, 2011. Yet he deceived a thirty-two-year-old Army veteran, who completed two deployments in Iraq and organized caravans of RVs to travel the country and pass out pamphlets on street corners.[60]

Camping also deceived a retired transportation employee who squandered his entire life savings of $140,000 to sponsor a NYC ad campaign. "I'm trying to warn people about what's coming," said Robert Fitzpatrick of Staten Island.[61] Ordinary, hardworking folks, well-educated adults, and ministers can all be duped by false prophets and teachers.

Jesus stated the danger in Mark 13:22–23: "For false messiahs and false prophets will appear and perform signs and wonders to deceive, if possible, even the elect. So be on your guard; I have told you everything ahead of time."

The apostle Peter also gives us characteristics of these imposters, saying "they will secretly introduce destructive heresies," and they "despise authority" and are "bold and arrogant" (2 Peter 2:1, 10).

Rebellion

The first characteristic false prophets or teachers display is rebellion. They will not subject themselves to authority and refuse to open their affairs to public scrutiny. If they do have associates or board members to whom they answer, these are not people of integrity nor do they hold the leader accountable. They are simply yes men. False teachers often face legal issues because they snub compliance with government agencies such as zoning boards, the IRS, or city and state officials.

Immorality

Peter warns, "Many will follow their sensuality" (2 Peter 2:2 NASB). They will display attributes such as "corrupt desire," "eyes full of adultery," and "lustful desires" (2:10, 14, 18). Although abuse and sexual misconduct may remain hidden for years, the truth inevitably surfaces.

Greed

Peter mentions a third characteristic of false teachers: greed. He wrote "In their greed these teachers will exploit you with fabricated stories" (2:3), and "They are experts in greed" (2:14).

These charlatans are compared to Balaam, "who loved the wages of wickedness" (2:15). Recall Numbers 22, which describes how Balak wanted Balaam to prophesy against Israel so he could defeat them. But Balaam was blocked by a talking donkey. Later, in Numbers 23 and 24, Balaam tried to curse the Israelites, but he could utter only blessings.

In NASCAR a red flag means all cars stop. Race officials then advise drivers where to park while serious accidents get cleaned up or dangerous weather conditions are allowed to pass.[62] Ask God to empower your pastors to spot the red flags of rebellion, immorality, and greed, which will reveal the false prophets and teachers.

Deceiving Spirits

The ability to know God's will is a critical element in a pastor's personal ministry and the ministry of the church. The apostle Paul warns, "The Spirit clearly says that in later times some will abandon the faith and follow deceiving spirits and things taught by demons" (1 Timothy 4:1).

The foundation for a Christian's guidance comes from the Bible, but the Word does not always give a specific course of action for a situation. Then we need to seek the Holy Spirit to be led onto his path.

In her book *A Christian's Secret of a Happy Life,* Hannah Whitall Smith cautions, "Many sincere children of God have been deluded into paths of extreme fanaticism, while thinking they were closely following the Lord the whole time. Remember, it is not enough to have a 'leading.' We must find out the source of that leading before we give ourselves up to follow it. Be careful not to be deceived!"[63]

First Corinthians 12:10 lists "distinguishing between spirits" as a spiritual gift. Neil Anderson, author of *The Bondage Breaker,* defines discernment as "that buzzer which sounds inside warning you that something is wrong."[64]

For those who don't have the spiritual gift of discernment, Hebrews 5:14 gives hope and instruction. "But solid food is for the mature, who by constant use have trained themselves to distinguish good and evil."

First John 4:1 tells us to, "Test the spirits to see whether they are from God." John then urges us not to trust any spirit that does not acknowledge Jesus Christ who came in the flesh as God.

In the last lap of a 1993 race at Talladega Superspeedway, Rusty Wallace's back bumper was smacked by Dale Earnhardt. Wallace's car went airborne, flipping end over end eight or nine times. Though many fans considered this to be the most horrifying accident they had ever witnessed, Wallace survived with only minor injuries. Afterward, car makers added roof flaps to the top of each stock car. These flaps are designed to keep the wheels on the ground when a car spins around. The flaps prevent the car from going airborne.[65]

As a protection for our pastors, pray they will remain in the Word daily. Then petition they will test and discern whether each nudging comes from The Holy Spirit or other dark spirits. We desire their feet to stay on the ground.

The Enemy Tries to Accuse

Our enemy not only deceives but also accuses. The accuser loves to soak us with discouragement about the failures in our spiritual service.

Mark Roberts, senior advisor of foundations for Laity Renewal in San Antonio, Texas, remarked, "Based on my experience, and that of so many other Christians I know, discouragement can be a powerful weapon in our enemy's arsenal."[66]

Rather than humbly confessing our sins (see 1 John 1:9), the devil wants us to fill our gas tank with inferiority.

The prophet Zechariah describes Satan in opposition to Joshua: "Then he showed me Joshua the high priest standing before the angel of the LORD, and Satan standing at his right side to accuse him. The LORD said to Satan, 'The LORD rebuke you, Satan!'" (Zech. 3:1–2).

In his book *The Bondage Breaker*, Neil Anderson describes Satan's accusations of Joshua against the backdrop of a heavenly courtroom. God the Father serves as judge while Satan acts as prosecuting attorney. Joshua, the high priest, is the defendant who represents all followers of God. Satan's accusations continue all day, every day. "But our defense attorney in heaven is Jesus Christ, and He has never lost a case," Anderson declares.[67]

Romans 8:34 explains, "Who then is the one who condemns? No one. Christ Jesus who died—more than that, who was raised to life—is at the right hand of God and is also interceding for us." Pray that our pastors will be repeatedly reminded of what Jesus Christ did for them.

The Enemy Tries to Rule

Some Christians wonder whether they can be demon possessed. Dr. Merrill Unger answers this question in his book *What Demons Can Do to Saints*. Unger states, "The demon enters . . . as a squatter and not as an owner or a guest or as one who has a right there. But he comes in as an intruder and as an invader and enemy. But come he does if the door is open by serious and protracted sin."[68]

Satan cannot rule us, but we can grant him control in our lives through our decisions to give in to temptation. Addictions come in a variety of packages: alcohol, binge shopping, gambling, drugs, overeating, and pornography are among the most common. Each one thrives on a vicious cycle of secrecy, succumbing to a craving, and shame.

H. B. London Jr. reported that during a single morning the office of pastoral ministry at Focus on the Family received five calls from pastors seeking help for addiction to pornography. One stated his struggle persisted for more than twenty years.[69]

Other more subtle addictions such as workaholism may not seem as bad but are just as devastating for the believer. Ask God to make Romans 6:14 real to your minister, "For sin shall no longer be your master, because you are not under the law, but under grace."

The Enemy Tries to Distract

Dr. Billy Graham recalled an incident in May 1959 when he preached to 4,000 students in Australia. As the evangelist told the Sydney University crowd about the necessity of faith, they all heard a sudden, loud bang and observed a puff of white smoke. Graham recorded the following in his autobiography, *Just As I Am*: "A figure appeared dressed in a flaming-red costume, complete with horns and a tail. When he walked up to me, I laughed and shook his hand. I took a small Bible out of my pocket, and with one hand on the zealous impersonator's shoulder, I outlined the Gospel to him."[70]

On the front page the next day, the *Sydney Daily Mirror* published a picture of Graham and the red-clad creature.[71] Although this appeared to be a prank, the interruption seemed to be an attempt to detour Graham from his preaching and the students from hearing the gospel.

The Enemy Tries Direct Attacks

Although the vast majority of Satan's attacks are subtle, sometimes he comes at pastors in a frontal assault. In Acts 13:4-12 Paul, Barnabas, and John Mark (called John, a helper, in this particular text) traveled across Cyprus proclaiming the Word of God in the Jewish synagogues. A proconsul, named Sergius Paulus, sent for Barnabas and Saul "because he wanted to hear the word of god" (Acts 13:7). But Elymas, a sorcerer, opposed them and tried to turn the proconsul (a Roman governor of a settled province) from the faith.

Verse nine tells us Saul was filled with the Holy Spirit before he looked straight at Elymas and spoke. "You are a child of the devil and an enemy of everything that is right! You are full of all kinds of deceit and trickery. Will you never stop perverting the right ways of the LORD?" (13:10). Saul then declared the LORD would blind Elymas completely but only temporarily. The proconsul believed when the sorcerer groped about and sought assistance from someone to lead him by the hand.

Safety Equipment

Toolbox

The HANS (Head and Neck Support) device in a race car restrains the head from snapping forward during an accident at speeds up to 190 miles per hour. The collar-style apparatus uses straps to connect to the helmet to prevent whiplash. Many drivers opted not to wear one because they felt it was uncomfortable. However, within hours of Dale Earnhardt's death, manufacturers received over forty orders. At the start of the 2002 season, NASCAR made HANS a mandatory piece of equipment for all drivers.[72]

Prayer: As Jesus did for Peter, will you pray a prayer of protection for your pastor?

Scripture: "Simon, Simon, Satan has asked to sift all of you as wheat. But I have prayed for you, Simon, that your faith may not fail" *(Luke 22:31–32)*.

James 4:7 relates a simple formula to use when under spiritual attack, "Submit yourselves, then, to God. Resist the devil and he will flee from you." I suggest all pit crew members memorize this verse.

Roger Barrier, pastor of Casas Adobes Baptist Church in Tucson, describes the nature of the attacks this way: "If I were the Devil, I'd wage warfare against pastors. I'd attack relentlessly with spirits of depression and despair, anger and bitterness, jealousy and lust, deceit and pride. I'd motivate all sorts of people and hosts of demonic forces to make pastoral life miserable."[73]

But believers and pastors don't need to cower and worry about impending attacks. We can prepare for them and employ the armor of God found in Ephesians 6:10–18.

Even as a NASCAR driver utilizes a helmet, specialized seat belt, and many other pieces of equipment for safety, an intercessor can pray each piece of the armor for their pastor's protection. The Appendix in the back of this book contains a prayer list for your pastor that walks you through each piece of the armor.

My Thoughts

I first met Vernon Maxted at a writer's conference in Kansas. Vernon spent sixty-eight years in pastoral and preaching ministry before he retired from his fulltime duties at First Baptist Church in Marshall, Missouri. At age ninety, he continues to serve in jail ministry, help with pulpit supply, and lead the Missouri Valley Baptist Association in prayer for revival. Reverend Maxted recently wrote to remind me, "Being called of God does not make any person more holy. It does make him, or her, a special target of Satan. Victories are won through prayer."[74]

Pastor Maxted's words encourage me to remain steadfast in my prayers for my pastors and have prompted me to warn all prayer warriors to stay alert as well. When we stand in support of our pastor in the prayer pit crew, we plant ourselves in the crosshairs.

While I wrote this chapter on spiritual warfare, I endured an intestinal virus and bacterial infection. My hard drive produced false error messages. A virus disabled my computer's security. These computer problems and illnesses may have been coincidences, but I took action and began a personal fast. I enlisted friends and family members to pray for me as I wrote. I recommend that you recruit faithful prayer warriors to intercede with you and for you.

John Piper, pastor of preaching and vision at Bethlehem Baptist Church in Minneapolis, concludes, "Unless you believe that he's going to win the war, you won't have the energy and the hope to sustain prayer for the triumph."[75]

These words echo what Jesus articulated in John 16:33, "I have told you these things, so that in me you may have peace. In this world you will have trouble. But take heart! I have overcome the world."

6

Peer Relationships

Over-the-Wall Guys

The Boy Scouts first sparked Robert "Red" Byron's interest in racing when they sponsored a soap box derby. During his childhood in Boulder, Byron delivered newspapers and shoveled snow from neighbors' driveways. He became an avid reader and kept a stack of Jack London books and *Popular Mechanics* magazines beside his bed.

At age ten, the curious redhead purchased a Model T Ford. He stripped his Ford down, subtracted the heavy fenders, strengthened the suspension, and souped up the engine. The soft-spoken Red began professional racing at age sixteen on a homemade track carved out of a local cow pasture. Byron won several local races before his career was interrupted by World War II.[76]

During the war Red Byron enlisted in the United States Army Air Force, where he served as a navigator and tail gunner. The Army sent Red to a military base in Alaska to recapture the Aleutian Islands. While his B-24 was under fire, two pieces of hot, razor-sharp shrapnel entered Red's left thigh and hip. Doctors suggested amputation, but Red refused because he needed his leg to race. After he nearly died from infection, anemia, and the loss of seventy pounds, Red spent the next two years in and out of surgery and convalescence. Thereafter, Byron limped while wearing a full-length leg brace bolted into an orthopedic shoe. He suffered continual pain.[77]

But his injury did not detour his driving. During his recovery, Red's sister encouraged him to buy a red Ford convertible. Byron designed a hand clutch and hired a local mechanic to install the doctored clutch in his convertible. His spirits lifted as he enjoyed the freedom of driving his Ford.

Byron's hankering for racing returned, and he shocked his family when he announced he wanted to compete again. Red, with the help of mechanic Red Vogt, configured a special clutch pedal for his weakened leg. At most races he needed to be helped into and out of his black V-8 Ford. He became part of the newly-formed Modified Series in which he won the first race at Daytona Beach. By the end of the year, Byron edged Fonty Flock by 32 points to win the $1,250 championship prize.

In 1949 Byron raced in NASCAR's Strictly Stock, which eventually became today's Monster Energy NASCAR Cup Series. Red Byron won his second stock car championship and became NASCAR's first champion.[78]

Racing experts agree that Byron's personal courage contributed to his success. Other Army comrades in his position took their pension and disability checks and retired to peaceful lives. But Red loved racing. He always carried an aspirin bottle and wolfed the pills like candy.

"He didn't complain . . . but you could tell when he was hurting sometimes . . . I'm sure he was in pain," said mechanic Frank Scott.[79]

Byron exemplified the first of NASCAR's professional drivers. Many other drivers came from bootlegging backgrounds, but not Byron. He knew he had to take care of his vehicle to finish the race. Byron recognized the necessity of driving under control and often passed former moonshine runners who had blown engines and tires. Red calculated how much fuel it took to run the number of laps in the race and filled his tank to that level. He understood weight and balance.

"Bootleggers knew one thing . . . pedal to the metal. And if you wrecked a car, it was just a wreck," commented Don Johnson, a mechanic for Byron.[80]

Red Byron secured financial backing from car owner Raymond Parks. Parks had left home at age fourteen to haul moonshine. A WWII veteran like Byron, Parks survived the Battle of the Bulge. After he served a nine-month prison sentence for a numbers racket, Parks became a legitimate businessman and made a fortune from vending machines and real estate.[81]

Red Vogt, known as a genius mechanic, fine-tuned Byron's car. Chief mechanic Vogt, a teetotaler like Byron, helped Ford design its cam shafts. He experimented with fuel additives and became known as an engine specialist because of the power he could pull from an engine.

Bill France, founder of NASCAR, invited Byron, Vogt, and Parks to the organizational meetings at the Streamline Hotel in Daytona

Beach, during which the rules for racecars and tracks were created. Red Vogt even suggested the name NASCAR, which stands for National Association for Stock Car Automobile Racing.[82]

Failing health compelled Byron to hang up his goggles in 1951. But he continued his involvement in racing. In 1960, he flew to Chicago for a series of meetings. Anheuser-Busch wanted to hire Byron for a new sports car team. In his Chicago hotel room, Red Byron died of a heart attack. He was only forty-five.

Experts credit Red Byron's success to his personal grit, his cerebral approach to racing, and the teamwork of driver, owner, and mechanics. The experience and expertise of the trio of Red, Red, and Raymond formed the best race team of the day.[83]

Peer Relationships

Like Red Byron, our pastors need a group of friends to support them and encourage them to finish the race (see 2 Timothy 4:7).

Parishioners assume their ministers, as church leaders, will enjoy dynamic relationships. But the Barna Group found 61 percent of pastors concede they "have few close friends."[84]

When we consider most churches in America employ only one pastor, the need for maintaining good friendships becomes critical. One of the first principles mentioned in the Bible is found in Genesis 2:18, "It is not good for the man to be alone."

Relationships between your pastor and members of the congregation may sometimes develop into friendships, but the relationship may be difficult.

John Ortberg, pastor of Menlo Park Presbyterian Church in Menlo Park, California, explains minister/member friendships this way:

> "Sometimes you may think of someone as a
> friend, but they are really only useful to you (like

people in your pyramid sales group). I sometimes think that relationships between pastors and folks in their churches are like this. It's not that friendships cannot develop between pastors and attendees; they do, and I've enjoyed a few myself. But there are dynamics of role and confidentiality and the desire for success that often complicate them."[85]

The apostle Paul mentions several friends who stirred his spiritual passion. Luke served as Paul's doctor, traveling companion, and much more.

In 2 Timothy 1:16, Paul referred to Philemon when he said, "Your love has given me great joy and encouragement, because you, brother, have refreshed the hearts of the Lord's people" (Philemon 7).

Aquila and Priscilla's home functioned as a rest stop for Paul. And Paul counted Titus a special friend when he wrote in 2 Corinthians 7:6, "But God, who comforts the downcast, comforted us by the coming of Titus."

Pray that our pastors will cultivate friendships with those who possess trustworthiness and integrity. No one wants a friend who is not dependable. A companion who lacks integrity may make your minister look bad.

Reverend William Ezell of Naperville Baptist Church explains integrity this way: "Integrity is not reputation (what others think of us) or success (what one has accomplished). Nor is integrity something we have; it is something we are that inevitably shows itself in what we do."[86]

Hurts remain an occupational hazard for those in the pastorate. When friends fail them, our shepherds may try to bear it and move on.

Proverbs 19:11 does tell us to overlook a small offense. But this verse does not apply to a major incident such as a betrayal. Over time, these emotional injuries grow and, if not dealt with, can lead to anger and bitterness.

H. B. London Jr. once commented that he sees too many of his colleagues develop a "'little black book' in their hearts filled with the offenses against them."[87]

Pray our pastors will drop all charges and forgive.

Each of our ministers requires a team of seven types of friends to keep them motivated and growing. These seven aspects of relationships form the acrostic FRIENDS. Sometimes one individual will serve as more than one type of friend. Ask the Lord to bring several friends into your pastor's life who will fulfill all seven roles.

Paul expressed his gratitude to Onesiphorus, "because he often refreshed me and was not ashamed of my chains."

F—Fun Friend

Every member of the clergy wants a fun friend. Jesus enjoyed several good friendships. Three siblings, Mary, Martha, and Lazarus, spent a tremendous amount of energy to provide Jesus an oasis of good food and relaxation at their home in Bethany (Luke 10:38–42).

In John 11, Jesus received a message saying that his friend Lazarus was gravely ill, but Jesus knew Lazarus had died. Jesus traveled to Bethany and found Lazarus was indeed dead. Scripture records that Jesus "was deeply moved in spirit and troubled" (John 11:34).

Later the Word states, "Jesus wept.

Then the Jews said, 'See how he loved him!'" (11:35–36).

Jesus raised Lazarus from the dead and enjoyed more time on earth with his dear friend.

John Ortberg meets annually with four fun friends at a cabin in the hills. They eat a grilled salmon dinner, laugh, share blessings and heartaches, and pray for an extended weekend. Ortberg comments: "Friendship happens . . . as a gift. It comes like rain or sunshine or

Cinnabons; a delight and joy and bonus that makes the world a better place. My friends are those people, those few and mysterious people, who love me for no reason at all. Which is the only really good reason to love."[88]

All preachers desire a companion with whom they feel at ease. They may share common interests. When they hang out, they recall the good times. They joke and laugh until their ribs ache. Fun friends are loyal and loving and want good things for their pal. Pray that our pastors find the fun friends they crave.

A—Reporter

After our pastors obtain a fun friend, they need a reporter. This is someone who tells them the truth about their attitudes and behaviors. It takes courage for our pastors to include a reporter in their circle of friends. Often their words hurt feelings or cause a sore, aching spirit.

The Bible says it this way in Proverbs 27:5–6. "Better is open rebuke than hidden love. Wounds from a friend can be trusted, but an enemy multiplies kisses." Reprimands or rebuke are difficult to endure but necessary.

Two issues are at work here. First, telling the truth is a rare commodity in our society. In many of our relationships, a friend will tell us a "little white lie" rather than hurt our feelings. If a friend does make a valid remark about our performance or approach, it may be done behind our backs. This is gossip and does not produce the reporting that will change our pastors' lives.

You've probably heard the old adage "Honesty is the best policy." This saying summarizes the principle found in Proverbs 28:23, "Whoever rebukes a person will in the end gain favor rather than one who has a flattering tongue."

A second issue is that many of us do not want to hear the truth. To handle an admonition in the right way can be tough. The pain may last for several days.

Clark Cothern, pastor of Living Water Community Church in Ypsilanti, Michigan, gave his trusted family members permission to tell him the truth about his conduct. Later, Cothern recorded his reaction to their comments. "Taking ownership of the truth is often a process with me. Even though I can hear it, understand it, and eventually accept it, it still takes a few minutes (or longer) for the attitude to catch up with the words coming out of my mouth."[89]

Mark 14:32–42 chronicles a well-known scolding. Jesus instructed Peter, James, and John to keep watch while he prayed in the garden. When the Lord returned, he found the three disciples asleep. Jesus asked Simon Peter why he could not watch and pray for an hour. This incident followed one earlier that evening in which Jesus revealed Peter would deny him three times. Peter insisted he would not disown Christ, in fact, he said he was willing to die with him.

In the garden, Jesus exhorted the disciples once again to watch and pray, but once more they fell asleep. The Lord resumed his prayer, then returned a third time to the disciples. He shouted "Are you still sleeping and resting? Enough! The hour has come. Look, the Son of Man is delivered into the hands of sinners. Rise! Let us go! Here comes my betrayer!"

A reporter is a valued friend. This person risks losing the pastor's friendship in order to advance the pastor's spiritual transformation.

"Rebukes are the purifiers which keep spiritual passion clear and forceful," states Gordon MacDonald, pastor emeritus of Grace Chapel in Lexington, Massachusetts.[90] Pray for a truthful and loving reporter for our clergy and that our ministers will respond with grace and action.

Tony Stewart's reckless behavior in his early years of racing earned him a bad-boy reputation. On his way to the 2002 NASCAR championship, he exploded into frequent emotional outbursts with his crew plus two altercations with cameramen. After a race in 2004, he shoved Brian Vickers in the chest and knocked the wind out of the rookie.

Driver Mike Wallace told Stewart he was "letting distractions get in the way of his accomplishments."[91]

The crossroads came when team owner Joe Gibbs called Stewart into the garage during the 2004–2005 off-season to talk with the crew. Gibbs intended to make his angry driver realize how these difficult blowups affected their work. Stewart said later he thought he would be fired.

But Stewart took the advice of Gibbs and his team. Although he was still a fierce competitor, Stewart became kinder off the race track. His relationship with his crew grew smoother. He related better with other drivers and reached out to fans.

After his 2005 championship, Stewart commented, "It's nice that they don't have to talk about my behavior anymore."[92]

Our pastors need reporters like Joe Gibbs and his team, who spoke honestly and lovingly with their friend, Tony Stewart.

I—Intercessor

In addition to a reporter, our pastors require two or three friends to serve as intercessors. The best example of intercession for another believer is recorded in John 17, where Jesus prays for his disciples (17:6–19). Then the Lord prays for all believers (17:20–26), which he continues to do from heaven.

Ron Edmondson, pastor of Immanuel Baptist Church in Lexington, Kentucky, gives this advice in choosing intercessors.

"You don't have to do it my way, but if you're a pastor, you need people you can trust praying for you in every area of your life. Yes, you need your entire church praying for you. I'm for more corporate prayer. I believe, however, that you need a smaller group around you to share more personal requests. When we look at the model of Jesus, He seemed to have that prayer support structure within the disciples, even calling a few of them frequently away from the Twelve to meet with him in more private settings."[93]

As you pray for your pastor, you may or may not be asked to be in the inner circle of intercessors. If you are tapped on the shoulder to be an intercessor, please be faithful. If not, please pray for those who are.

"A Christian fellowship lives and exists by the intercession of its members for one another," wrote Dietrich Bonhoeffer, "or it collapses."[94] Bonhoeffer, a Lutheran minister in Germany during WWII, was arrested by the Gestapo and later executed April 9, 1945, for preaching, teaching, and writing about Christ. He understood the value of intercessors.

Gordon MacDonald suggests church members intercede with praise, needs, and protection. Petitions for spiritual passion, renewal, not becoming weary, and equipping for spiritual warfare are vital.[95]

At age ten, I overheard my mom tell my dad her prayers for our pastor were being answered. Parishioners who complained about our minister's "boring" sermons had stopped their complaining and had joined her in prayer. At the time, I did not understand the significance of this conversation. The power of my mom's intercession for her pastor and fellow believers brought harmony to our little country church.

E—Encourager

The fourth type of friend our pastors need is an encourager. While the reporter tells our pastors what is not right, an encourager affirms what they are doing well. The encourager observes and then comments on the worthy actions and attitudes of eternal value. For young preachers, positive evaluation is essential so they know what they need to continue.

Tool Box

In a maneuver called drafting, NASCAR drivers race in single file to share the air flow among their cars. The first car creates a vacuum effect that actually pulls the car behind it. Cars cut through the air much faster together than they do separately. Drafting also conserves fuel, which can result in fewer pit stops and more wins on the race track. Several years ago Jamie McMurray and Juan Pablo Montoya of Earnhardt Ganassi Racing became drafting buddies. The synergy helped both McMurray and Montoya run faster.[96]

Prayer: Pray that your pastor will find a buddy who will help him or her with the burden of ministry to finish the race and complete his calling.

Scripture: "However, I consider my life worth nothing to me; my only aim is to finish the race and complete the task the Lord Jesus has given me—the task of testifying to the good news of God's grace" *(Acts 20:24).*

Some may think pastors should get their positive strokes from God, not from men and women. A quick look at Scripture demonstrates otherwise. Paul encouraged the believers in Thessalonica when he said, "And so you became a model to all the believers in Macedonia and Achaia" (1 Thessalonians 1:7).

Paul also praised Philemon for his love and faithfulness and prayed for Philemon (Philemon 4–5).

Ministers go through periods of hard work, sometimes only to receive critical letters, emails, or social media messages, often delivered anonymously. Such harsh criticism can drain your preacher or bring on an inferiority complex. While a pastor sorts out any truth in these communications, it is vital to have an encourager with plenty of praise.

The saying, "Patting a fellow on the back is the best way to get a chip off his shoulder,"[97] has been repeated so many times no one knows the original author.

But the ultimate pat on the back came from God the Father after Jesus' baptism, which is recorded in Mark 1:9–11. When Jesus left the water of the Jordan River, heaven opened and God said, "You are my Son, whom I love; with you I am well pleased." Pray for an encourager to keep your pastor free from discouragement and passionate about serving.

N—New Blood

Besides a fun friend, reporter, intercessor, and encourager, pastors require new blood in their contact lists. A new blood is a friend who puts aside his or her own personal agenda or goals to partner with the pastor. This partner helps share the load of ministry and inspires the pastor to get the most out of his energy.

The apostle Paul had a number of such partners and clearly did not want to be without them in his life and work (see 2 Timothy 4:9–13, 19–22). Luke, Barnabas, Silas, John Mark, Timothy, and Titus assisted Paul as comrades in spreading the gospel.

At age twenty-three, George Beverly Shea composed "I'd Rather Have Jesus." In 1943, while poised for a successful career as a composer and musical artist, Shea instead signed on with Billy

Graham as a singer. Many other roles followed during the next sixty years as Shea, who was ten years older than Graham, served on the evangelistic team. Shea became known for his good sense of humor.

One of the funny stories he shared with Jerry Jenkins, author of the Left Behind series, involved a young couple who kept staring at Shea at Chicago's O'Hare International Airport. The man came up to Shea and asked if he sang for Billy Graham. When Shea confirmed he did, the man hollered to his wife, "Honey, come here! It's George Beverly LaHaye!"[98]

Pit to Pulpit

Elijah was a man of God who needed a friend. While chased by Jezebel, Elijah became exhausted and isolated. At this point, he cried out to God that he was the only committed servant left. After God revealed there were seven thousand faithful people in Israel, he sent Elisha to be Elijah's servant and friend (see 1 Kings 19).

Prayer: Ask God to bring a fellow seminarian, a church leader, pastor, or other believer to be your pastor's loyal friend.

Scripture: "A friend loves at all times, and a brother is born for a time of adversity" *(Proverbs 17:17).*

After Graham developed Parkinson's disease, his dear friend made every effort to attend special events. A few team members noticed Shea sat next to Graham at dinner and discreetly cut his meat for him. George Beverly Shea passed away on April 16, 2013, at age 104.

Pray for a loyal, humble new blood like Shea to energize and lend a hand to your pastor.

D—*Discipler*

The discipler (or mentor) is the sixth friend every minister of the gospel requests. Disciplers are especially needed by younger pastors. A discipler is different than a new blood.

H. B. London Jr. explains the distinction this way: "The important aspect of mentoring is not using a protégé to accomplish the mentor's goals. Rather, it is a process by which the one being mentored becomes all that he or she should be."[99]

Disciplers serve in the roles of cheerleader and coach, but not critic. They give feedback, answer questions, and are open about their own struggles and how to deal with them. A mentor wants your pastor to succeed and functions as a good role model.

Pastors may desire a discipler for a variety of reasons. Early in his first pastorate, Gordon MacDonald realized that his tendency to avoid conflict was hurting both his marriage and ministry. He wrote, "I searched out mentors to learn how to be a man of greater candor. To know how to confront the associate who was under my organizational authority. To learn how to rebuke the person who needed firm pastoral influence. To master the ability to speak my heart to my young wife in a way that would not hurt her or tear at her self-confidence."[100]

Many young pastors report they have sought out a mentor but were refused because the would-be discipler was too busy. Indeed, discipling does take a considerable amount of time, but the lack of mentors is a terrible hindrance to building Christian leaders.

Women in ministry report they have even more difficulty finding disciplers. After her inability to obtain a mentor, Sharon Predovich founded Women's International Minister's Network (WIMN) in order to train women for ministry. Predovich and her husband, Bill, co-pastor Resurrection Life Church and World Ministry Center in Eden Prairie, Minnesota.[101]

Gordon MacDonald's wife Gail explains her disciplers tend to be dead people. She writes, "I found them in the great biographies where I was able to discover the hidden secrets of great men and women of God. It's not quite the same, but it helped a lot when there were no older, more experienced people who were willing to provide me with the time I needed to grow.[102]

Pray for more veteran ministers to free up their schedules and be available to mentor upcoming pastors.

S–Shepherd

The shepherd is the final necessary friend for a pastor. A shepherd demonstrates tenderness and comes alongside a pastor during a season of sheer exhaustion or crisis. This individual helps make sense when life becomes confusing and possibly fearful. A shepherd can assist when trauma keeps a minister from thinking clearly or being able to act decisively. The shepherd's function is to lead, feed, and protect.

Paul exemplifies a shepherd in Acts 27. The apostle was then a prisoner who was being taken to Rome to stand trial before Caesar. While on a ship to Italy, a fierce storm of typhoon strength began to blow. The ship was battered by the wind to the point it could not be controlled, so the crew dropped anchor to keep from running aground. The crew did not eat for several days and threw cargo overboard to lighten the ship. But when they saw neither the sun nor stars for days, they gave up all hope.

Paul gathered the ship's company and announced, "I urge you to keep up your courage, because not one of you will be lost; only the ship will be destroyed" (Acts 27:22). He explained how an angel of God had revealed the truth to him. Due to his faith in God, Paul was able to tell the crew to take courage, knowing they would be protected.

When the sailors realized they were close to an unknown shore, Paul challenged everyone to eat. Paul gave thanks for the food and ate some bread. The passengers followed his example. At daylight they saw a sandy beach, but the ship ran aground before they reached it. Anyone who could swim was ordered to jump in and head to land while others used pieces of lumber from the ship to float to safety. All 276 reached the beach without harm.

Like the crew members in Acts 27, your pastor will need a shepherd to turn to during a time of trouble. This distress may come in the form of a loved-one's death, the diagnosis of a serious illness, or a life-threatening accident. Pray for someone to walk with your pastor during his time of crisis.

Most of us still remember February 18, 2001 as the horrific day when Dale Earnhardt died during a last-lap crash at the Daytona 500. Just five months later, NASCAR fans wondered if his son, Dale Earnhardt Jr., would be able to enter the Daytona stadium. The week before the race, Dale Jr. took some friends with him to tour the track. He wanted to see if he could handle being there. He was okay.

With his father's death looming over the track, Dale Jr. led 116 of the 160 laps and won the race. His win caused riotous merriment in the stands. In no hurry to go to Victory Lane, Junior pulled into the infield to allow his teammates and crew to gather around him. Family friends, bus drivers, and guys from the team stood in the parking lot and recalled the turning points in the race.

Earnhardt noticed fellow driver Dale Jarrett stood to his right. When he asked why he was there, Jarrett replied, "I wouldn't miss this for the world."[103]

Ten years later, Dale Jr. remembered the excitement of his competitor when he won the Daytona. He considers Jarrett a good friend and explains, "That was the best part of the whole deal."[104] Everyone needs a good friend during a tough time.

Fun friends, reporters, intercessors, encouragers, new blood, disciplers, and shepherds support our clergy during both joyful and troubling seasons. Both periods can be a time of growth with the help of a few good friends. Pray your minister never has a lack of close friends.

7

The Pastor at Home

Racing Families

A number of colorful drivers were involved in NASCAR's early years. The Flock family, who lived in the Atlanta area, stole the hearts of many fans. Of the four brothers and two sisters, four raced in NASCAR events.[105] Brother Bob won the pole for NASCAR's first sanctioned race in Charlotte.[106] In 1947 and 1949, Fonty won national stock car championships.[107] Tim Flock exceeded them all when he became the 1952 and 1955 Grand National Series

Champion, and he holds the record for the highest career winning percentage for a full-time NASCAR driver (21 percent).[108]

Ethel Flock Mobley raced in over one hundred NASCAR events during her career. She competed mostly in the Atlanta area. Named after the high-test gasoline of the time (ethyl[1]), Mobley drove her Cadillac to an eleventh-place finish at Daytona in July 1949. She finished ahead of brothers Bob and Fonty. Tim took second place.[109]

Carl Flock raced boats. Reo, who was named after the car of that name, enjoyed an elevated sport. The youngest in the family, she performed skydiving and wing walking.[110]

All of the Flocks were involved in the family business, illegal moonshine. Fonty delivered bootleg liquor on his bicycle before he started driving routes. He reminisced, "I used to deliberately seek out the sheriff and get him to chase me. It was fun, and besides we could send to California to get special parts to modify our cars, and the sheriff couldn't afford to do that."[111]

When brother Bob drove onto the track in Atlanta to begin a race, federal agents followed him. Police chased him around the track several laps before Flock plowed through the fence. The pursuit continued until Bob ran out of gas. He later recalled, "I would have won that race if the cops had stayed out of it."[112]

Ministry Spouses

Like the Flock brothers and sisters, the pastor's immediate family members also become a part of the family business. Many

---

1. In the early 1900's internal combustion engines developed "knocking" due to the out-of-sequence detonation of the gasoline/air mixture in the cylinder. Two General Motors chemists developed tetraethyl lead to stop the knock. Ethyl, the world's first anti-knock gasoline, became popular with motorists. Its added power proved to be vital for aviation engines in World War II. Because of the safety concern of the lead, engines were improved, new additives were discovered, and ethyl gas was banned in 1986 by the EPA.

congregations consider the minister's spouse and children a part of the pastoral team even though they don't have a nameplate on a door.

Christine Hoover's husband, Kyle, is a church planting pastor in Virginia. Hoover surmises: "I wasn't good at geometry proofs, but it seems to me that if a = b and b = c, then a = c. If I'm called to this man, and he's called to this work, then I'm called as well. My role in our ministry looks totally different, but I'm called to it just the same."[113]

Identity and Priorities

In an informal survey conducted in 2013, Thom Rainer asked the question: "What do you wish you had been told before you became a minister's wife?"

The most frequent response in this open-ended query was: "I wished someone had told me to just be myself."

One respondent stated, "I am a people-pleaser by nature, so for me, not being prepared to handle being a pastor's wife with my personality was a heavy burden to carry early in our ministry."[114]

Sometimes ministry spouses are nudged into roles that are not a good fit with their talents, gifts, and passions. When a pastor accepts a new position at a church, the spouse often looks for a place of service that is unfilled and within his or her giftedness.

This was evidenced in a respondent's answer to a *Leadership Journal* survey:

> "After my husband and I entered our first pastorate, I was asked to sing, play the piano, or teach young children. Since I am not musically inclined, I decided to teach beginners. I figured this class might be suited to me since I was a beginner myself. After a while I graduated to the junior high,

where I remained for six years. I loved the boys and girls, but I still felt unfulfilled. Finally, after all those years of being pushed and pulled into roles I was not particularly suited for, I discovered I had the gift of teaching young marrieds. I finally felt the satisfaction that comes when you are doing what you feel God has called you to do."[115]

Other pastoral mates allow their position to define their lifestyle and identity. When their identity wraps around the label of Mrs. Pastor or Pastor's Husband, they must figure out what this role requires and how to fulfill it. This can leave the spouse open to expectations to serve in the same way as last minister's spouse. In the process of "finding oneself," a danger lurks. The husband or wife may take on too many responsibilities.

One morning, Jane Rubietta found herself in this spot as she prepared to run errands. When her husband asked her to run a few errands for him while she was out, she exploded with angry words. Rubietta grabbed a high chair and slammed it into the floor.

She said, "Something had gone terribly wrong with my soul. My quiet time was no longer nurtured. So busy being indispensable, I had crowded out God. Equating value and identity with productivity kept me working harder, longer, trying to endear myself to others and, perhaps, even winning God's approval."[116]

Pam Morgan, former pastor's wife at First Church of the Nazarene in Wichita, Kansas, shares how she found reason in her role.

"As a people-pleaser with the middle-child syndrome, I find myself always wanting to be happy and get along with everyone. So I've found balance in turning to God's Word, because ultimately I'll answer to the Lord. My desire must be to please Him above all else. I've made Psalm 19:14 my life prayer: 'May the words of my mouth and the meditation of my heart be pleasing in your sight, O Lord, my Rock and my Redeemer.'"[117]

Pray that clergy spouses can quiet the noise of expectations, both real and imagined. Ask God to help them find their identity in Christ and follow his promptings that match their created designs. May our pastors' wives and husbands find peace, joy, and confidence in their service as they fully follow their Lord.

Oswald Chambers writes in the November 13 entry in *My Utmost for His Highest*, "How can anyone who is identified with Jesus Christ suffer from doubt or fear! It ought to be an absolute paean of perfectly irrepressible, triumphant belief."[118]

No pastor's spouse can be Magnificent Mom, Hero Husband, or Mrs. or Mr. Church. Intercede for our ministers' spouses to be able to prioritize their lives with God first, then family, and finally their ministry.

Reverend Robertson McQuilkin served as president of Columbia Bible College and Seminary (now Columbia International University) from 1968 to 1990.[119] In a chapel service, he stood before the Columbia students and announced his resignation so he could offer full-time care for his wife, Muriel. Mrs. McQuilkin had supported her husband in ministry for forty years until she weakened with Alzheimer's disease. Robertson took care of her until her death in 2003.

Many ministry friends urged him to continue "God's work" and put his wife in a nursing home.[120] McQuilkin objected, saying, "It's a great honor to care for such a wonderful person." Of the major decisions he's had to make, he claimed caring for Muriel was "one of the simplest and clearest."[121] The McQuilkins exemplify a family who knows how to prioritize their lives.

Boundaries

I called Angie, but had to leave a message when there was no answer. I put my phone down and returned to my chores. The phone startled me when it rang before I could flip the switch on my vacuum cleaner.

"I'm sorry I didn't pick up your call. But I have to let calls go to the answering machine on Saturday mornings. Gary is out picking up kids for practice."

"No problem, Angie."

"They keep calling. They want to know when he's going to be there."

This was the first time I witnessed an intentional boundary set by my friend to keep her family's sanity. I wondered what other boundaries youth pastors' spouses enforced.

This demonstrates one of the many ways ministry families deal with trying to keep their family time sacred. Living in a glass house, as some have described it, can be a detriment to family privacy.

In her book, *I'm More Than the Pastor's Wife*, Lorna Dobson defines these parameters. "Boundaries are simply limits to protect us from being overcome by things that are not in and of themselves evil but are 'opportunities' that can drain our effectiveness."[122]

These boundaries can be tough when the pastor's family has a small group meeting in their home. Boundaries can be breached when a crisis happens outside office hours and the phone rings at home. This situation grows more dicey if pastoral housing is next to the church.

I know of one parsonage that is attached to the church building making it possible for parishioners to walk from the church lobby into the family living room.

Ministry families experience the same struggles every other family does—plus they deal with being in a fish bowl under constant scrutiny. A pastor's family needs a safe haven and a quiet place for downtime. Burnout can take hold if home is as hectic as the office and as draining as ministry.

Kay Warren, pastor's Wife at Saddleback Church, once said you know you're too busy when:

- "You have not emptied your mailbox in three days.
- You walk in the door and the dog growls at you because he doesn't recognize you.
- Your pots and pan have cobwebs on them.
- You use your bathtub as a planter.
- The guy at the drive-through window at Taco Bell knows you so well he's willing to loan you money."[123]

Donna Alder and her husband are both ordained ministers and have served for over thirty years. She developed a questionnaire which was administered to pastors' spouses at two retreats. When asked what they disliked the most about the ministry, 47 percent answered "expectations others have of me."[124]

Expectations can be overt or veiled. A congregation may expect the current ministry spouse to take on all the responsibilities held by the previous spouse. Expectations can vary from congregation to congregation. Therefore, it becomes important to pray these expectations will be clarified at the start of a new pastorate.

Early in her husband Ross' ministry, Carol Rhoads wrestled with the stress and pressure of what some church members perceived her role to be. "When I shared my concerns with Ross, his response was very reassuring.

"He said, 'Honey, you're the pastor's wife, not the church's wife.' That wise statement provided more freedom for me than can be imagined."[125]

Like Pastor Rhoads, clergy can make family members feel special rather than a second fiddle to God's work. Jerry Falwell encouraged the "preacher boys," as he called the pastoral majors at Liberty University, to follow his example in setting up a calendar. The first four events scheduled each year were his anniversary and the birthdays of his children.

During the early days of building Thomas Road Baptist Church, Falwell's wife, Macel, commented, "Jerry, I've seen far too many ministers take care of everyone else's children to the detriment of their own."[126]

A similar standard was found in a *Leadership Journal* survey of minister's wives. One respondent commented:

> "I know one minister who dates his wife on a regular basis. Even their children know on one particular night each week their parents have a date. When something comes up, the husband simply says he has an important commitment that cannot be broken. He and his wife feel this has made a major difference in their relationship, as well as a big impact on their children, who see their parents' authentic love and respect for each other."[127]

I wonder if the wife, who wrote this response, wished her husband would do the same.

Reverend Frank Schaefer posted this joke on his website. "Pastor's spouse: 'Honey, let's reverse things on this Sunday morning. You'll be nice to us and grumpy to the congregation.'"[128]

As we chuckle, we realize it is difficult for ministers not to come home and dump the frustrations of the day on their dear families.

Counselor Diane Langberg gained an up-close view of many church leaders' marital issues at her private practice in Philadelphia. She states, "One of the most important assets in an effective ministry is a healthy and strong marriage. Many people in ministry are failing God because of problems in their homes generated by their neglect."[129]

In addition to fun times together, the ministry family needs to spend devotional time together.

During an interview with *Ministry Magazine,* Willie and Elaine Oliver stated, "Leaving a spiritual legacy to our children is among the best gifts we could ever give them as ministry leaders—the kind of gift that will stay with our children for many years to come."[130]

Pray for your pastor's family to schedule fun activities and devotional times together. Intercede that these times will not be pushed aside by "more important" events.

NASCAR driver Jeff Gordon knows how it feels to be placed on a pedestal. Gordon has won the championship for the Winston Cup Series (now Monster Energy NASCAR Cup Series) four times. Driver of car number 24 earned NASCAR Cup victories in ninety-three races, which makes him third on the all-time wins list.[131]

However, in 2002 Gordon's headlines changed from victories to court proceedings. His wife at the time, Jennifer Brooke Sealey Gordon, declared their marriage of seven years "irretrievably broken" when she filed for divorce.[132] After the break up, Jeff Gordon explained the source of his healing when he posted the following on his website:

"I welcomed God into my life a few years ago and I regret that I did not do it sooner. Embracing faith has made a tremendous difference in my life and my overall well-being. Motor Racing Outreach has also been a part of my life. Their mission is to introduce the racing community and its fans to personal faith in Christ. MRO helped me to develop and continue my relationship with God."[133]

If your pastor and spouse experience a rough patch in their marriage, pray they will seek and find help (professional counseling if necessary) to resolve the issues and heal the brokenness.

The apostle Paul reminds us, "Be completely humble and gentle; be patient, bearing with one another in love" (Ephesians 4:2).

Intercede that church leadership and the congregation will be supportive of the pastor's family. Ask God to help your minister and spouse develop a good marriage that will serve as an example to their children, their church, and their community (see Ephesians 5:22–33).

Pit to Pulpit

In a major research study of senior pastors in Protestant churches, researchers found 10 percent have been divorced."[134]

Prayer: Ask God to bring an individual(s) to help your pastor's family walk through their difficulties.

Scripture: "And Saul's son Jonathan went to David at Horesh and helped him find strength in God." *(1 Samuel 23:16).*

Friends

Ministers cannot meet all the relational needs of their spouses. Occasionally, the spouse needs some girl- or guy-time with good friends. Friends can be found among other ministry families. In the community, the spouse may make friends with a parent on their child's soccer team. He or she might become a pal with someone who enjoys the same hobby. A pastor's spouse could also find friends in his or her church.

Loneliness and the need to find good friends is a consistent problem with clergy spouses. Colleen Evans's husband, Louis, served in a renewal ministry of the Menlo Park Presbyterian Church.

She recommends three steps to finding a good friend. First, she suggests a minister's spouse should pray for God to lead him or her to someone they can trust. Next, Evans advises the spouse to look for someone who displays emotional health and maturity. Finally, she says to "dare to be transparent."[135]

Pray for your pastor's spouse to find a friend as faithful as Jonathan was to David. "After David had finished talking with Saul, Jonathan became one in spirit with David, and he loved him as himself" (1 Samuel 18:1).

Licensed psychologist Diane Langberg says she frequently fields questions from ministry spouses about how to find good friends, why some in the congregation shy away from the pastor's spouse and why others play up to them. Those who pull away seem to place the pastor's spouse on a pedestal. The members who work hard to gain the ear of the ministry spouse appear to set themselves up in some sort of power play. Langberg says, "I believe that the answer lies largely in the fact that many women in the congregation see you as a role and not as a person. You are not Jane or Sally; you are the pastor's wife."[136]

In a *Leadership Journal* survey of clergy wives, 56 percent said they do not have close friends in the church. Twenty-eight percent reported this was intentional. One respondent related this story:

"A couple in the church we were at before we went into the ministry became very involved with their pastor and his wife. They would go out every Saturday together. They were so close as to exclude and neglect others in the church. It caused much jealousy and resentment. Eventually, the problem became so intense it caused the pastor and his wife to leave the church. Seeing this happen made me very cautious in forming friendships in our own church."[137]

Lorna Dobson, in her book *I'm More Than the Pastor's Wife*, mentions another complicating factor, which she calls culture shock. Dobson describes culture shock as loneliness and disorientation experienced by a clergy spouse. These feelings can result from moving across the country away from relatives and friends.

A pastoral family who leaves a small town for a ministry in an inner city will certainly feel this. A new ministry in the Northeast can make a family from the South feel out of place. While mission organizations spend considerable time preparing their candidates for culture shock, Christian colleges and seminaries teach no such assimilation skills for ministry here at home.[138]

Moving can exhaust even the heartiest soul. Some denominations move their clergy every two to five years. Muriel Phillips, whose husband served as pastor of the Norwich and New London, Connecticut, Seventh-day Adventist churches, comments on moving. "While some may look on this activity as a grand adventure, I do not find it enjoyable. In some circles, moving has been regarded as a 'way out,' or a 'way up.'"[139]

In *Tips for Ministers and Mates*, author Mary Bess challenges readers to focus on the positive aspects of moving. She lists three benefits:

- The opportunity to get rid of accumulated clutter
- Having a wardrobe that is "new" to the new church
- The opportunity to make new friends and experience new growth[140]

Intercede for your minister and his or her family to leave their previous church on a high note. Pray for your pastoral family as they adjust to a new church and community. Ask God to guide them in getting comfortable with new situations and friends.

Macel Falwell did not have to deal with moving, because her husband, Jerry Falwell, founded and remained pastor of Thomas Road Baptist Church until his death in 2007. Jerry was fascinated by the frolics of his wife Macel's circle of seven friends.

Her bunch met for lunch, gave baby showers for each other, and traveled together. These gals stayed friends for years until Macel's friend and traveling companion, Shirley, succumbed to cancer. Later, a second friend died of cancer. Macel couldn't stand the thought of losing another friend.

Each year she invites the gang and together they schedule their mammograms. She explains, "With the right attitude you can have fun doing anything, including having mammograms. If anyone misses her appointment, I don't rest until it's been rescheduled and I know she's suffered through hers like the rest of us. Fair's fair, after all."[141]

Although Macel Falwell had five other friends to lean on when she went through a tough time, some ministry spouses do not have a close friend to help them.

Donna Alder, in her questionnaire of pastors' spouses, found 88 percent of her respondents admitted to having "experienced periods of depression."[142] Please pray your clergy's spouse will find good friends who can support him or her through these difficult seasons.

Contentment

Besides tearing ministry spouses from their friends, moving can also cause discontent. If the ministry family loves the church, their family's home, and their community, then it becomes difficult to pack up and leave. The wife or husband has become nested in the family's current place. Moving turns into a hassle when you enroll the kids in new schools, find new doctors, dentists, and individuals to do repairs. Selling the family home can develop into a long process and bring on financial problems if the pastor's family has to reduce their asking price to hasten the sale. Turning on the utilities and paying the deposits adds further financial stress. A church member who helps with moving may drop Aunt Sue's antique vase. The item may not be valuable, but it represented a multitude of special memories.

Nancy Pannell describes one difficult move she experienced:

> "Part of my grief in leaving Tulsa was leaving our arbor. This may seem like a silly, inconsequential thing, but that arbor represented a sort of haven for me, and leaving it symbolized leaving the security of my known world. Would you believe, the first house shown to us, as we began to look for a new home, had a wonderful arbor over the back porch!? Would you believe, the owners reduced their asking price, making the house affordable for us!?"[143]

Lack of financial support can also be a factor in making a ministry spouse dissatisfied. Many small churches are unable to provide a full salary and benefits, so clergy in these congregations must obtain employment outside the church. Bivocational church planters such as Terry Dorsett usually work a full-time job while they launch their new assembly of believers. Dorsett says bivocational pastors may feel pulled in two different directions, and spouses may complain of their mates' never being home. Even though they may provide only a part-time salary, many congregations still expect their minister to be on call twenty-four hours a day. The pressure can be overwhelming. Exhaustion and burnout are common.[144]

Some researchers estimate as many as 30 percent of ministers in the United States are bivocational.

Ralph Kelly, pastor at Good News Church in Colorado Springs, says of his wife, Daisy, "If she wasn't as flexible and giving as she is, I wouldn't be able to succeed as a bivocational minister."

He and his wife make family their first priority. "We also set aside some family time, usually each week, that nothing can displace. Daisy and I work hard at staying in tune with our four children."[145]

Closely related to this issue is the fact that many pastors' wives must work to make ends meet. Sometimes these working women are misunderstood by people in the pew who think these spouses value career more than the church.

One wife of a church planter in Ohio said, "No one seemed to 'get it'—that I was working, because many were not being faithful to God's call to tithe."[146]

Another tough issue is deciding when to retire. In most churches, there is no mandatory retirement age. Athletes in nearly every sport struggle with this issue. A number stay too long and play a mediocre or dismal last season. Likewise, preachers sometimes stay too long and their energy level, as well as their congregation, dwindles.

Joyce Williams prayed about retirement for two years before she and her spouse both sensed God wanted him to retire on his sixty-sixth birthday.[147]

Pray pastors and their families will realize that God will provide their needs. Ask the Lord to move in the hearts of their congregants to be sensitive to the financial needs of their minister's family. Pray that our Heavenly Father will help each family member to be gracious and thankful when they receive these blessings.

Poor health or difficult pregnancies are other issues which can rob pastoral spouses of their joy. The weakness, pain, and uncertainty that accompany medical issues can demoralize and create financial problems. Prayer is the power that will sustain the spouse. Ask God to heal and bring them through. Pray they will have opportunities to share their faith as they work through health issues.

Criticism

The Great Commission commands us to make disciples of all people. Church leaders and members passionate to fulfill this mandate differ over the methods to use. Unfortunately, these disagreements can sometimes turn ugly. A minister's spouse may be attacked for his or her suggestion of a particular evangelistic event. Generally, the difference of opinion is not the problem, but an ill-thought reaction can be.

Pray that the spouse will have the patience and grace to follow the advice given in Proverbs 15:1: "A gentle answer turns away wrath, but a harsh word stirs up anger."

Such situations can develop into an opportunity to examine motives, check for harmful attitudes, and deploy scriptural principles of resolution. Pray that your minister's spouse will meditate on Psalms 139:23–24 which says, "Search me, God, and know my heart; test me and know my anxious thoughts. See if there is any offensive way in me, and lead me in the way everlasting."

Constructive comments could be an occasion for growth and esteem. Proverbs 13:18 records, "Whoever disregards discipline comes to poverty and shame, but whoever heeds correction is honored."

Some criticism is unjust and of a more personal nature. Once a pastor's spouse determines her or his conscience is clear, then the spouse may want to explore the reason for the attack to better understand what faces them.

Professional counselor Diane Langberg says that a church member may feel the spouse "infringes on her territory." Perhaps she sees herself as the one who people go to when they have a problem but resents the pastor's wife when others go to her instead.[148]

A second possibility is when the individual bears a grudge against all authority figures. This scenario can be confirmed if the previous spouse or others in church leadership also received critical remarks. Petition the Lord for wisdom and discernment as your minister's mate deals with harsh or untrue criticism.

Lorna Dobson, in her book *Caring for Your Pastor*, relates that while they were in a store shopping, an unfamiliar woman approached her husband Ed. "'Well, I'm glad you got a haircut; now I can finally listen to the sermon!' Then she walked away.

We shook our heads and later we both wondered, 'What is she really angry about?'"[149]

Many ministry spouses find it much more difficult to deal with faultfinding that is aimed at his or her family. Pastor's wife Carol Rhoades remarked: "Perhaps the most difficult thing I faced was hearing undeserved criticism about my husband. Some was constructive, but there were instances when mean-spirited people who were jealous gossiped and hurt us deeply. Without our faith and ironclad commitment that we continue to reaffirm daily, we would most certainly have given up."[150]

Criticism can be delivered in some awkward methods. Lorna Dobson studied music in college and plays piano. Parishioners would approach her with their analysis of the music and want her to pass on their evaluation to her husband.

Another second-hand approach happens when critical mail or anonymous letters are sent to the home. Many spouses dislike serving as the messenger of bad news. Instead they prefer keeping the home an oasis. Sometimes the preacher's children are asked by church members to pass on information to mom, which is to be relayed to the pastor in a third-hand fashion.[151]

Pray for your pastor and the pastor's family for insight to know how to deal with these thorny situations. Exercise James 1:5 in your prayer. "If any of you lacks wisdom, you should ask God, who gives generously to all without finding fault, and it will be given to you."

Husbands and wives can also be tempted to step in and try to take up an offense for a family member. God transforms peoples' lives through tough times, according to Proverbs 20:30, "Blows and wounds scrub away evil."

Intercede that the pastor's spouse won't interfere as God works, and for wisdom parents need to guard children from harassment.

In addition to criticism and gossip, a betrayal can sting deeply. Betrayals squeeze the heart until all strength drains. Disloyalty paralyzes. When a trusted friend goes behind the back and divulges information meant to be kept secret, a deep wound develops. Forgiveness needs to be applied immediately.

"Get rid of all bitterness, rage and anger, brawling and slander, along with every form of malice. Be kind and compassionate to one another, forgiving each other, just as in Christ God forgave you" (Ephesians 4:31–32).

Pastor's wife Meredith Floyd loves to teach women's Bible studies. After she was hurt by a friend, she noticed an anxiety welled up and tightened her chest when the individual was around or the person's name was mentioned.

Meredith recalls: "My experience with unforgiveness lasted over a year, and God really used this entire situation to teach me just what can take root in our hearts after being hurt. Truly, unforgiveness can lead to great bondage and has the potential to spill over into every part of your life. On the other hand, giving the gift of forgiveness brings great freedom!"[152]

Ask God to help your minister's spouse to be gracious and forgiving when others expect too much, behave with unkindness, misunderstand, or evaluate in error.

Jeana Floyd's husband, Ron, pastor of First Baptist Church of Springdale and the Church at Pinnacle Hills in Springdale, Arkansas, made the front page of the newspaper and was the lead story on the local evening news during a controversy. Jeana became uncomfortable when she went out in public. One night they both attended an athletic event at the local high school.

> "I noticed a lady staring intently at my husband as we approached the ticket gate. She was dressed in noticeably tight clothes and puffing away on a cigarette. She began to approach us and I braced myself for a tongue lashing right there in public! As she got closer, she said, 'Aren't you that Ronnie Floyd?'
>
> 'Yes, ma'am,' my husband replied kindly.
>
> The next words out of her mouth completely amazed me. 'I wish the media would just leave you alone. You just keep preaching the Word.' Then she turned around and walked off! Needless to say, I was speechless and extremely relieved! That was probably God's way of telling me to ease up and quit worrying!"[153]

Sometimes God will bring encouragement from unexpected places if we pray for our pastors and their families.

Support

Along with encouragement, support is very important for the ministry spouse. At a ministry conference, 58 percent of pastors' wives reported "support and encouragement of my husband" as their most important role.[154]

Many people in our society are hostile to authority. They grew up without anyone in their lives to look up to. As a way to survive, they learned to look out for their own rights and gave little value to the rights of others. Their experience consisted of leaders and people of influence who mistreated them, ignored them, or treated them inconsistently or unfairly. Because of this background, they assume all individuals in authority behave the same way. Their theory of authority causes them to lash out at bosses, teachers, police officers, pastors, and others whom they perceive to have clout.

Ministry spouses encounter a tough job when they try to encourage and support their pastor in such difficult circumstances.

In an open-ended survey, one ministry wife stated, "I need to be his cheerleader. Dealing with critics in the church is difficult. He needs to hear that I respect him now more than ever."[155]

Tool Box

NASCAR can be a dangerous sport. Some drivers will not climb into their car until someone prays for them. Others slide a cross into their pockets before the race. Stevie Waltrip, wife of Darrell Waltrip, encouraged her husband and other drivers who needed a boost. Prior to the starting of the engines, she attached Bible verses to the dashes of their cars.[156]

Prayer: Pray that our pastors will be supported and encouraged by their spouses to remain faithful to their callings.

Scripture: "Tell Archippus: 'See to it that you complete the ministry you have received in the Lord'" *(Colossians 4:17).*

Another ministry spouse supports her husband in this way: "My husband is on the firing line of anger, jealousy, bitterness, and pain every day. It is my main function to make home a peaceful place to be."[157] A pastor who leaves an oasis each morning starts his or her day in the best way possible.

To be a haven, the home requires a vibrant marriage. Pray spouses will remind themselves what attracted them to their sweetheart and how they will treasure their life's mate. Love can be demonstrated in many ways, such as kind and affectionate words, giving gifts, sharing intimacy, spending time, serving, and showing honor.

Jeana Floyd mentions this important distinction about loving your spouse. "Recognize the difference between saying 'I love you' and 'I'm in love with you.' 'I love you' means I choose to love you. 'I'm in love with you' means I think about you, talk about you, want to be with.' Ministry marriages need both—the deliberate choice and the 'I can't help myself.' Let your husband know you are 'in love' with him."[158]

Most pastors' spouses see themselves as best friend and lover. They also agree prayer remains top priority. Some pastors' spouses work diligently to make Sundays as stress-free as possible. Clothes are washed, dried, and organized. Meals prepared. Sleep and nap times protected. They strive to keep a good attitude when they need to be away and encourage the kids to do so as well.

Ministry wife Stephanie Wolfe articulates her support of her husband:

"I love my job as the Head Minister to the Minister. I'm responsible for that smile on his face when he walks confidently to the pulpit. I'm responsible for that spring in his step when he heads into the church office. I'm responsible for that dapper suit and tie he is proudly wearing. I'm responsible for that good attitude that helps him face disgruntled members or difficult counseling situations. I have a big responsibility and I take it seriously, because you see, my minister-husband isn't complete without me. He needs me. He needs my hugs and kisses, and pats on the back, and cheers, and smiles, and 'amens!' Well, call me arrogant; but quite frankly, I feel like I'm important to the whole project. You see, I go with him everywhere he goes, even when I don't leave the house!"[159]

Preachers supported by their spouses can find ministry a joyful partnership. But who supports the spouse?

Joe McKeever, who served for forty-eight years in ministry as a pastor and director of missions, states, "No one in the church family is more vulnerable than the pastor's wife."[160]

He feels pastors' wives are under-appreciated for what they do to promote the health of the church. They sit on the firing line of criticism and also watch their husbands and kids under attack. Yet they are expected to not fight back and bring a delicious casserole to the next church dinner.

Jena Fellers supports her husband, Steve, at Trinity Worship Center in Baxter Springs, Kansas. Trinity is a small church with a large feeding ministry. Jena wrote the following in her journal.

Why Pastors Need Prayer—July 2nd

"It was a crazy morning on the last day of June which landed on a Sunday, and not just because of the jungle-looking decorations on the platform and down the sanctuary walls. Yes, Steve knew it was the day for VBS's program so things wouldn't be normal. He also knew it was the Sunday before Independence Day, and he had recorded a special song with video to play before his sermon was to start. But his day started much earlier than that. First he had to run to Wal-Mart to buy party favors for me to use in Children's Church to remind the kids of the story, The Prodigal Son. From there he went on to the church to turn air conditioning on and check bathrooms to ensure toilet paper and paper towels were in abundance. He had an extra chore of removing sixty cases of food from the Children's Church room to avoid yelling from me. After he accomplished this task he went to the bathroom where he ended up fixing a stopped-up toilet.

Now it was finally time to do his normal Sunday morning events like typing the church bulletin with all the announcements and prayer requests and to make sure his video would work. Naturally some of those coming in for Sunday school stop to ask a question here and there. Then the music minister likes to go over songs with him since he plays the guitar. During this process Leslie came in quickly and urgently, 'Dad, come clean up Elijah's mess. He just threw up in my class.' Off Steve went to clean up puke from four-year-old Elijah who appeared to be well upon his arrival, but soon went home. That mess finally cleaned and I had to remind him to run home to grab our hose and nozzle so after church the VBS leader could be sprayed by the eager boys who gave more offerings than the girls. When water is involved, no one can resist the temptation to soak Steve. So his front was drenched-tie and all. Welcome to Pastoring 101."[161]

Jena, an ordained minister herself, experiences more difficulty supporting her husband than most ministry wives because she is visually impaired, only able to see shadows. Her white cane indicates her challenge. However, many pastors' wives face adversity that cannot be seen. Ministry spouses encounter confidential situations they cannot reveal. Those of us in the pews are unaware of the pressures that confront them. They need us to intercede to a God, who knows and sees all. Prayer is a spring that never dries up.

Preacher's Kids

David Reutimann raced the number 83 Toyota Camry for BK Racing during 2013. He began his career racing in dirt-track modifieds and late models. Reutimann was named Rookie of the Year in the Craftsman Truck Series in 2004. Michael Waltrip Racing signed him to drive in the NASCAR Sprint Cup Series (now the Monster Energy NASCAR Cup Series) for the 2007 season.[162]

Reutimann is a third-generation racer. He is the son of Buzzie Reutimann, who made one NASCAR start in 1963. Buzzie, a legend on the dirt-track circuit on the East Coast with over 1,200 wins, gets requests for his autograph almost as often as his son. Father and son, Buzzie and David, are well known for their close relationship. Cameras have spotted them behind Reutimann's hauler laughing and teasing each other on numerous occasions.

Ty Norris, vice president and general manager of Michael Waltrip Racing, feels David wants his father to share in his NASCAR experience. "It's unbelievable how close they are. They're rare. I've never seen anything like it."[163]

Unfortunately, some preachers' kids don't experience the sweet relationship the Reutimanns do. Due to the constant meetings and demands of the ministry, some PKs rarely see their fathers. Ministry kids report how demoralized they are when dad or mom is called away for a congregational emergency just before their basketball or volleyball game.

One PK recalls how the whole family was awakened when her father received a call at three o'clock in the morning to come pray for a parishioner who had an itch that wouldn't quit.[164] PKs experience pressure from unrealistic expectations, bullies who criticize, pressure to perform, and family issues.

Expectations

Expectations for a minister's child can far exceed what is expected of children whose parents have professions.

Take, for example, these sentiments received by the Billy Graham family when Franklin was born:

- "Welcome to this sin-sick world and the challenge you have to walk in your daddy's footsteps."
- "May his great father's mantle fall on him."
- "Dear Little Billy Frank, Jr. we heard . . . that your Daddy has new help for preaching God's truth. Praise the Lord! So grow up fast."
- "Good luck and best wishes to the young preacher."
- "Countless thousands of us are rejoicing and thanking God for your birth."[165]

Even though these are extreme examples, nearly all preachers' kids report feeling pressure to be better students, have superior character, and possess exceptional holiness. In response to the pressure put on ministerial parents, pastors and their spouses sometimes burden their children with unrealistic expectations as well.

When called upon to pray at every youth meeting, PKs feels called to a higher standard. They think their lives are being played out on a stage under the spotlight. The danger is they may grow up associating their faith with impressing other people instead of God.

Kyle Idleman, teaching pastor at Southeast Christian Church in Louisville, Kentucky, recalls the pressure of being a PK. "Growing up I often did all the right things not primarily out of love for Jesus but because I knew people were watching, and I cared what they thought. Inevitably this leads in one of two directions: to hypocrisy (you embrace the stage and become a professional actor), or to rebellion (if people want a show, you'll give them a show). For many ministry kids it leads to both, rebellion that no one knows about."[166]

God wants PKs to be obedient and respectful with no appearance of being rebellious, but He never demands they be perfect.

Pray these verses for ministry kids. First Timothy 3:4 says this about anyone serving as an overseer or deacon: "He must manage his own family well and see that his children obey him."

These words are found in Titus 1:6, "An elder must be blameless, faithful to his wife, a man whose children believe and are not open to the charge of being wild and disobedient."

Church Bullies

Another problem some PKs face is church bullies. A pastor's seven-year-old son looked forward to the Sunday school assembly where each week the boys and girls would sing "Happy Birthday" to their friends who had birthdays the previous week. However, one week the children's department director skipped the birthday recognition because he was angry at the pastor about a decision he had made. What better way to show his spite than to crush the pastor's son's spirit.[167]

A preacher's daughter commented, "There's no mean like church mean." What terrible injustice had come her way?

Although bullies are a small minority in any church, the emotional harm they cause is despicable. Please pray for protection for ministry children so they will be treated with kindness and encouragement.

Prodigals and Rebels

The teenage years are tough for most young people. Teens typically deal with identity issues and loneliness. This issue multiplies exponentially for ministry teens. Finding their identities muddles with the expectations of others. If a church member has hurt them, they may struggle with trust issues. Some may hide behind a mask and pretend everything is okay while others may act out.

One way PKs stage a silent protest against this treatment is to leave the church (meaning to never participate or attend) once they are on their own. In a survey of 600 such PKs, several reoccurring themes surfaced. These included:

- Having harsh and dictatorial parents who allowed little freedom
- Parent(s) who placed higher priority on their work than on their home
- Hypocritical parent(s) who behaved one way at church and another at home
- Physical, mental, or (in a few cases) sexual abuse by parent(s) or church members[168]

Please pray ministry children will be able to forgive the people who have hurt them in the past. Ministry children, even after they become adults, may need courage or a softening of their hearts to enter counseling. Ask God to help them trust again. Also pray for clergy who are parents so that they can guide their children to a love for the Lord and his people.

Some PKs are more openly rebellious. If you know many pastors' families, you may hear of scenarios similar to these: Police call to inform the preacher his teen has been arrested. A nurse from the ER phones for treatment permission after a drunk driving accident or a drug overdose. A pastor's daughter announces she is pregnant, or a son admits his girlfriend will soon have his child. As a son leaves town, he explains he wants to be with his homosexual lover. These acts have huge consequences for both the teen and her or his family.

Pray for ministry teens to realize and face the results of their bad choices. Intercede so parents and the congregation will display love and forgiveness and will always keep the door open for a repentant PK.

The prayers of Billy and Ruth Graham were answered for their son Franklin. In his book *Rebel with a Cause*, the oldest Graham child owns up to his wild-driving, gun-toting, cigarette-smoking, and Scotch-drinking days.

Reflecting on his experiences, Franklin Graham came to a realization: "I was catching on to the fact that people expected me to be some kind of example and would hold me to a higher standard. I thought this was unfair, and to some extent I still do. But it was reality, and I needed to start getting used to it. One thing never changes: With privilege comes responsibility."[169]

Family Problems

Family problems can also trouble a preacher's kid. Parents or siblings may become seriously ill. Financial woes may cause pressure. Ministry kids may be deeply saddened by their parents' separation or divorce. The death of a particularly close grandparent, aunt, or uncle can be disheartening. Some pastoral parents conceal serious issues like these for years and never deal with them. Parishioners may assume the smiling, happy ministry family at church functions the same way at home.

Funny girl Chonda Pierce's family sang and performed joyfully in church programs, but lived a nightmare at home. Pierce grew up with a family secret: her dad struggled with manic-depression. His mental illness became so bad, one night he came to her bedroom door with a revolver in his trembling hand. He told Chonda and her younger sister he was going to end it all but they should not be afraid when the gun went off. She lay awake for hours waiting for the firearm to discharge. That sound never came because Chonda's mother talked her husband out of taking his life.

For years their family appeared normal and happy in public. However, their family situation came to a boiling point when Chonda was sixteen. Her older sister was killed in a car crash on slippery pavement. Chonda's father, overwhelmed with grief, left his ministry and family. Chonda's older brother married and moved away. Not long after, her younger sister passed away, shortly after being diagnosed with leukemia. In less than two years, Chonda's family had downsized from six to two.

People laugh so hard tears stream down their faces when they hear Chonda perform a comedy routine. Many are shocked when they learn of her heartbreaking background. Humor became her mask, her way out of excruciating pain and grief.

After she married her childhood sweetheart, David Pierce, she returned to the hope of her Savior. She speaks and laughs about her experiences to groups all over the country, and tells her story in her book *Second Row, Piano Side*.

In her book, Chonda Pierce talks about the woman she calls Aunt Doris. Chonda, the middle of three sisters, felt left out on many occasions. Aunt Doris, not a relative, let Chonda sleep at her house. She cooked her favorite foods and took her shopping for candy and bubble gum on Saturday afternoons. Aunt Doris made Chonda feel special.[170]

Pray for an Aunt Doris to enter the lives of the PKs in your church.

The Positives

Being a PK carries both positives and negatives. Most ministry children do survive the high expectations and pressure to perform. Along the way, they learn coping skills. Suffering forges their character. While their parents talk with people after services, PKs chat with various members of the church and learn communication skills with individuals of all ages. Pastor's kids develop empathy at an early age as they watch their parents help people going through difficult times.[171]

Many former PKs relate numerous joyous experiences, such as personally meeting and interacting with guest speakers, participating in church programs, discovering their own gifts and talents, and seeing their dad as a respected member of the church and community.[172]

Two brothers mentioned the best thing about growing up as the preacher's kids was sneaking into the church late at night, cranking up the sound system, and pretending to be rock stars. PKs enjoy the leftovers from potluck dinners. Their command of King James English helps them when they study Shakespeare in school. By bench-pressing their parent's set of exhaustive biblical commentaries, they can build bulky muscles.[173]

Keep praying for your ministry families. Pray ministry parents will demonstrate how to:

- navigate the scrutiny and expectations placed upon them
- deal with criticism
- make trustworthy friends
- find their identity in Christ
- and determine their God-given purpose

Pray the PKs will grasp these concepts and incorporate them into their lives.

A good number of these kids will follow in their parents' footsteps and will pursue a career ministering to people. In many cases, these young people will become the future leaders of our churches.

8

Physical and Emotional Health

Yellow Flags

―――――◆―――――

WINNING WISDOM

Finally, we can no longer escape the realization that the ministry of intercession requires time of every Christian. ... Because intercession is such an incalculably great gift of God, we should accept it joyfully. The very time we give to intercession will turn out to be a daily source of new joy in God and in the Christian community.
DIETRICH BONHOEFFER

―――――◆―――――

A t age five, Trevor Bayne started his racing career. He raced go-carts for eight years, and during that time he won three world championships. Bayne then competed in the Allison Legacy Race Series and the USAR Hooters Pro Cup Series. He was awarded top rookie honors in both. Dale Earnhardt Inc. hired Bayne and placed him in their driver development program in 2008.

In the 2009–2010 season, Bayne raced for Michael Waltrip Racing. He raced for Roush Fenway Racing from 2010 to the present except for part of the 2011 season with Wood Brothers. Bayne raced during the 2014 season in the Nationwide Series. Roush Fenway invited Bayne to race in the Sprint Cup Series for the 2015 season. In 2011, he became the youngest driver to win the Daytona 500, at the age of twenty years and one day.

Later in 2011 Bayne was hospitalized for a spider bite. After the hospitalization he reported numbness in his arm. After a five-week hospitalization, Bayne announced he had contracted Lyme disease.[174]

November 12, 2013, Bayne shocked the racing world with another health scare. After undergoing tests at the Mayo Clinic, he announced he had been diagnosed with multiple sclerosis.

The twenty-two-year-old told reporters, "My goals are the same as they've been since I started racing. I want to compete at the highest level, and I want to win races and championships. I am in the best shape I've ever been in and I feel good. There are currently no symptoms and I'm committed to continuing to take the best care of my body as possible. I will continue to trust in God daily and know that His plan for me is what is best."[175]

Trevor Bayne is an outspoken Christian and has been on several mission trips to Mexico with Back2Back Ministries.

Godwin Kelly, the author of Bayne's biography, *Driven by Faith*, said, "This is a star being born. Trevor is cut from the same cloth as people like Tim Tebow. He works hard in everything he does and isn't afraid to let people know he's of the faith without pushing it on them either."[176]

Health Issues

Like Trevor Bayne, pastors may face serious health problems. Here are two recent examples and one from church history.

Illness Case 1

Terry Dorsett, Connecticut church planting catalyst for the North American Mission Board, was diagnosed with colon cancer in March 2014. His doctor scheduled surgery the following week.

Dorsett posted on his Facebook page, "Doctor said I should expect to spend the next few weeks shifting from the bed to the couch to the bathroom. Oh . . . Joy . . . That fits my personality well." He normally does an early-morning prayer walk each day.[177]

Family and friends were concerned that Dorsett's down time might get him down. They were thrilled he was adapting well when a few days after surgery he wrote, "I used to have a colon, now I only have a semicolon."

Recent tests indicate he is a cancer survivor.[178] Dorsett's biggest issue now is wondering why he is well while a dear friend who worked alongside him as a church planting missionary in Vermont is slowing losing her battle with cancer.[179]

Illness Case 2

Attorney Charles Finney became a Christian on October 10, 1821. The next morning he went to his office and told his client, "I have a retainer from the Lord Jesus Christ to plead his cause, and cannot plead yours."[180]

He prepared for the ministry and was ordained in 1824. The Female Missionary Society of the Western District hired Finney and sent him to the frontier communities in upper state New York.

At Evans Mill, Revivalist Finney preached several evenings about wickedness without allowing for any response. His messages were more of a lawyer's argument than a preacher's sermon. The next meeting, after his remarks, Finney asked attendees to publicly declare their faith in Christ.

The church erupted with some standing to their feet, some falling to the floor on their faces, and some groaning or bellowing. After several more nights, Finney continued the same pattern in a nearby town, then another and another. Each time large numbers of congregants responded in a similar fashion.

The highpoint of Finney's preaching came in Rochester, New York, where he presented sermons over ninety-eight evenings. Shopkeepers closed their businesses, posting notices urging people to attend Finney's meetings. Reportedly, the population of the town increased by two-thirds during the revival, and crime dropped by two-thirds over the same period.

A year later, the revivalist leader of the Second Great Awakening was forced to curtail his traveling after he contracted cholera. He spent the remainder of his life as a pastor of three churches and served as a theology professor and president at Oberlin College.

Some church historians call Finney the father of modern revivalism and feel he paved the way for future mass-evangelists such as Dwight L. Moody, Billy Sunday, and Billy Graham.[181]

Illness Case 3

In fall 2000, Ed Dobson, who was serving as senior pastor of Calvary Church in Grand Rapids, Michigan, was diagnosed with ALS, better known as Lou Gehrig's disease. Doctors told Dobson he had two to five years to live and that most of that time would be in a disabled state.

Since then, Dobson has written *Prayers and Promises When Facing a Life-Threatening Illness*, *My Year of Living Like Jesus: My Journey of Discovering What Jesus Would Really Do*, and *Seeing*

Through the Fog: Hope When Your World Falls Apart. Dobson also wrote and filmed seven segments in a project about hope called *Ed's Story.* The film trailer includes the following dialogue.

> Every human being knows they're going to die. The difference is I feel it with every twitch in my muscles. I feel it in the depths of my being.
>
> And, I realized that I was really dying because I had given up. When you're living in fear, every issue is overwhelming.
>
> ALS forced me into a situation where I grew in understanding what it meant to obey Jesus. I think early on in my life, I thought I was in control. And the truth is: you don't control squat.
>
> One day it will be over. But it's not about how long I have left, it's about how I spend the time I do have.[182]

Ed Dobson died on December 26, 2015, fifteen years after his diagnosis.

Pit Prayers for Health Issues

Knowing how to pray for our pastors who have serious or terminal illnesses can be difficult. We would wish for a miraculous healing, which would give our ministers an opportunity to witness about God's love and power. This is apparently the scenario of Terry Dorsett.

However, God may pit our pastors, like Charles Finney, for a time of reflection in which they may discern how God wants them to change the direction or nature of their service. Many preachers have expressed how pain and brokenness can also reveal small, hidden areas of their sinful nature our Father wants changed. Pastors' sicknesses may also lead their congregations, families, or friends to pray more.

At other times, God allows a serious, debilitating malady and fuels his servant with grace for the journey. Seeing a joyful individual amid the most grueling of circumstances baffles sinners and saints alike. We can only conclude the grace of God resides in that person's life. Ed Dobson's experience with ALS fits this category.

Some illnesses move into remission, then return or worsen. This scenario can wear on both patient and prayer warrior. Be prepared to pray for the long haul. Also, do not forget to pray for family members and close friends who are also on this ride. Do not presume what God may be doing in and with an individual's life.

Toward that end, recall these verses to pray for a pastor who has a serious illness. Remember to focus your prayers on the Healer and not the healing. Also, realize heaven may be the Father's choice of ultimate healing.

- Pray that our pastors will not become discouraged but will immerse themselves in the Lord. "For the joy of the LORD is your strength" (Nehemiah 8:10).
- Ask God to heal the pastor if it is his will. "For I am the LORD, who heals you" (Exodus 15:26).
- Intercede that your pastor will not experience unbelief, doubt, or fear when he or she has bad reports and obstacles. "Don't be afraid; just believe" (Mark 5:36).
- Pray family members, friends, and medical staff will believe in Jesus and deepen their relationship with him. "This is good, and pleases God our Savior, who wants all people to be saved and to come to a knowledge of the truth" (1 Timothy 2:3–4).

- Ask God to send encouragers (both people and the Holy Spirit) when the pastor experiences pain, discomfort, and misery. "May my prayer come before you; turn your ear to my cry. I am overwhelmed with troubles and my life draws near to death" (Psalm 88:2–3).
- Intercede that our pastors will draw near to God with a pure and holy heart. "Let us draw near to God with a sincere heart and with the full assurance that faith brings, having our hearts sprinkled to cleanse us from a guilty conscience and having our bodies washed with pure water. Let us hold unswervingly to the hope we profess, for he who promised is faithful" (Hebrews 10:22–23).
- If any evil spirits are connected to this illness, then pray in the name of Jesus that they will be bound. "Jesus said to him, 'Away from me Satan!' . . . Then the devil left him and angels came and attended him" (Matthew 4:10–11).
- Ask that your pastor will not fear death but will have peace and hope. "And free those who all their lives were held in slavery by their fear of death" (Hebrews 2:15).
- Pray to the Lord that your pastor will receive mercy and grace to sustain him or her through the process. "Three times I [Paul] pleaded with the Lord to take it away from me. But he said to me, 'My grace is sufficient for you, for my power is made perfect in weakness.' Therefore I will boast all the more gladly about my weaknesses, so that Christ's power may rest on me.'" (2 Corinthians 12:8–9).
- Ask God to fill your minister with strength, power, and endurance. "He gives strength to the weary and increases the power of the weak" (Isaiah 40:29).

Heart Breaking Issues

Pastors face issues other than health. Their own emotional problems or of those close to them can put them in a tailspin. Depression, anxiety, and other mental illnesses are prevalent in our world and occur in ministry families. Let's review a few cases.

Depression Case 1

For thirty-eight years in London, Charles Haddon Spurgeon was the pastor of New Park Street Chapel, later called Metropolitan Tabernacle. As a preacher well known for his rousing oratory, Spurgeon also penned a prolific number of books, commentaries, weekly sermons, magazines, poems, and hymns.[183]

At age twenty-two, Spurgeon's congregation grew so large they rented a music hall for Sunday worship. On June 7, 1891, while Spurgeon was praying, someone from the overflow crowd falsely yelled, "Fire!"

Although it was unclear whether the individual was an enemy of Spurgeon, a prankster, or an emotionally disturbed person, seven people were killed and many more were injured in the scramble to escape. Spurgeon collapsed and was so distraught he had to be helped from the pulpit. He slipped into a deep depression, which he later wrote and spoke about in lectures and sermons.[184]

Depression Case 2

Bibb Mount Zion Baptist Church in Macon, Georgia, led by Reverend Teddy Parker, has 800 members. One Sunday morning in 2013, Parker's family and congregation anticipated his arrival to preach. When he did not show up, his wife and two children searched for him. His wife discovered his body in the driveway of their home. Reverend Parker had committed suicide.

His family later disclosed that Parker had been on medication for manic depression. Apparently he needed to take a break from ministry but felt the church would not allow it. Reverend Parker did not know how much to share or how much grace would be extended to him.[185] He suffered from a wound that did not bleed or leave a scar. His sore ached far worse.

Pit to Pulpit

Fifty percent of pastors say they are unable to meet the demands of their jobs and are so discouraged they would leave the ministry if they could. But they have no other way of making a living.[186]

Prayer: Pray that your minister will not lose heart and will focus on victories rather than problems.

Scripture: "Therefore, my dear brothers and sisters, stand firm. Let nothing move you. Always give yourselves fully to the work of the Lord, because you know that your labor in the Lord is not in vain" *(1 Corinthians 15:58).*

Depression Case 3

In another example of depression, Minister Art Greco stopped at a stoplight on his way home for lunch. Suddenly everything around him became unfamiliar. He wanted to be alone, which was strange for him. He scored extremely high as an extrovert on the Meyers-Briggs Type Indicator.

Greco continued slowly down the street, looking for something familiar. He turned left a couple of times when it seemed to feel correct. He found the block he thought he lived on but didn't know which house was his. Greco pushed the button on the garage door opener. When a door opened, he pulled into the driveway. He decided to keep this experience to himself. Not even his wife knew.

A few days later, his doctor diagnosed stress-induced depression and recommended he change professions.

Greco said, "I was afraid that people would see me as weak that the stresses of planting a church and functioning as pastor were too much for me. I wasn't going to tell the church's leadership; I wasn't going to tell my wife; and I sure wasn't going to tell my superintendent. Pride convinced me that I would be branded if anyone found out. But, thankfully, keeping my secret eventually turned out to be impossible."[187]

As Greco's condition worsened, his wife, close friends, and church leaders saw through his cover-up and asked probing questions. The leaders of his church helped by seeking a doctor's second opinion and offered to help him follow the recommendations.

Ministers Parker and Greco are two of many pastors who deal with depression. Another emotional issue pastors may suffer is anxiety.

Anxiety Case 1

David Trig went for a run in Palm Springs, California, when the temperature was 110 degrees. Trig, a pastor for over fifteen years, was overcome with fear to the point he grabbed onto a palm tree. After several minutes of thinking he was having a heart attack, wondering if he would live, and other terrifying thoughts, he calmed himself and made his way home. He spent the next ten years learning how to deal with his own anxiety. Now, Trig ministers as an anxiety coach.[188]

Anxiety Case 2

In his book *Walking on Water When You Feel Like You're Drowning*, Tommy Nelson, pastor of Denton Bible Church in Denton, Texas, describes a similar experience:

"Thirty minutes before the evening service, just as I always did, I was conversing with people and waiting for the service to begin. From nowhere, in an instant, all my strength went out of me. My body went limp in the chair, my heart rate skyrocketed, and my blood pressure rose so high that I could feel my entire body shake. I wasn't sure what was happening. I went to my office and lay down on a couch. In about fifteen minutes, everything subsided, and I went out and preached. I noticed that afterward I had an unquenchably dry mouth. Something wasn't right. I went to the doctor, who had me hospitalized. I eventually learned I was having an anxiety attack or panic attack."[189]

After his attack, Pastor Nelson's anxiety continued like a "persistent toothache." Reading became difficult because he was unable to concentrate on the page. His joy in reading the Bible diminished to the point that Nelson could never stay on subject for more than thirty seconds. He went to his elders and told them he was "toast" and unable to carry on as usual. Nelson asked for three months' rest, which was granted by his board. He saw a psychiatrist to take care of the physical aspects of his condition and went into counseling to help with day-to-day practical issues.

Other Issues Case 1

Pastors face a number of emotional and family issues in addition to depression and anxiety, which can be equally heart wrenching. Megachurch Pastor Ron Carpenter has been married for twenty-six years and has three children. In October 2013, he stated from the pulpit of Redemption World Outreach Center in Greenville, South Carolina, that his wife had entered psychiatric treatment.

Carpenter's wife had created a completely separate, dual life apart from their relationship. In her alternate life, Mrs. Carpenter committed multiple acts of adultery. Of her own volition, she checked into a one-year rehabilitation clinic, where she was kept in isolation for evaluation. Therapists told Carpenter it was "the worst case they had ever seen."[190]

The following February, after much prayer, counseling, and medical treatment, Hope Carpenter sat on the front row at church with her family, where congregants applauded her return.[191]

Other Issues Case 2

Another pastor's heart breaker came when his sixteen-year-old daughter handed him a note on Valentine's Day weekend. It read, "I am gay. I am happy this way. And if you really love me, you won't try to change me, and you will not try to talk with me about this." This ministry couple struggled through sleepless nights, embarrassment, and many fears. They were scared they would be rejected by their friends, afraid their daughter's depression would lead to suicide. They also feared their daughter might not rekindle her walk with the Lord. Even though their faith has been tested, they are closer to God and love their daughter more than ever.[192]

Tool Box

Davey Allison was NASCAR's Rookie of the Year in 1987 and won the Daytona 500 in 1992. In 1993, he was killed in a helicopter crash at the Talladega Superspeedway infield.[193] His wife, Liz, spent some time healing but has returned to her passion for NASCAR. She is now involved as a member of the sports media, covering the sport in print, radio, and television.[194]

Prayer: Think of a pastor who has gone through a traumatic experience. Pray for his or her healing.

Scripture: "But for you who revere my name, the sun of righteousness will rise with healing in its rays. And you will go out and frolic like well-fed calves" *(Malachi 4:2).*

Other Issues Case 3

The Purpose Driven Life author Rick Warren and his wife, Kay, described to CNN anchor Piers Morgan how they "stood in the driveway, just embracing each other, sobbing." Meanwhile, police officers searched Matthew Warren's home after his parents were unable to reach him.

Matthew had attempted suicide before. The Warrens sought the finest specialists, top-rated hospitals, and the best treatment available. Matthew received much love, support, and prayer. After many misdiagnoses, Matthew's condition was finally identified as borderline personality disorder.

The family's worst fears were realized when, following twenty-seven years of seeking help for his mental illness, Matthew killed himself with a firearm he bought online.

"Matthew was not afraid to die. He was afraid of pain," Rick Warren told the TV cameras on *Piers Morgan Live.*[195]

The leadership of Saddleback Church gave the Warrens a sixteen-week sabbatical. Rick Warren then returned to the pulpit and shared his thoughts on 2 Corinthians 1:3–11 in what may have been the most-viewed sermon in history. He followed that with a message series entitled "How to Get Through What You're Going Through." Kay shared her stint with hopelessness as well.

For years, counselors have treated grieving counselees based on the four stages of grief identified by Swiss psychiatrist Elisabeth

Kübler-Ross in her 1969 book, *On Death and Dying*. These stages over the years were expanded to seven and then shortened to five.[196]

In his preaching series, Rick Warren introduced the Six Stages of Loss: shock, sorrow, struggle, surrender, sanctification, and service. The Warrens have also been spokespersons to raise awareness for mental illness and other issues.[197]

HELP!

Some argue that the Bible is all you need to recover from mental or emotional difficulties. However, this did not work for Pastor Nelson, whose anxiety kept him from concentrating on the scripture pages in front of him.

Some find medication helpful but are dismayed that the drugs mask a part of their personality.

Minister John Colwell explained the effect after being treated with lithium. "My mood stabilized, life became manageable. Imagine the horror of my physician when . . . I announced that I wanted to stop taking the tablets. They made me feel truncated." Colwell has not taken lithium in thirty years. Instead, he dug into the Psalms of lament and developed strategies for coping.[198]

Many couples, like Ron and Hope Carpenter, find counseling valuable. Pastor Greco reluctantly submitted himself to his doctor and church leadership for recovery. Some preachers, like Spurgeon and the ministry couple whose daughter was gay, have found emotional issues will teach and lead to a deeper walk with God.

Pastor Trig and the Warrens found emotional and mental issues opened the door to new avenues of ministry. Nearly all individuals with mental illness and their families deal with shame and stigma from church members, friends, and neighbors who do not understand or even fear emotional issues.

In 2 Corinthians 11, Paul enumerated many of the physical afflictions he endured including beatings, hunger, thirst, imprisonments, stoning, exposure to cold, sleeplessness, and a shipwreck. He concluded his list of sufferings in verse 28. "Besides everything else, I face daily the pressure of my concern for all the churches."

Reverend Parker seemingly felt overwhelmed by the burden of tending to his flock and left his responsibilities behind for someone else. Shepherding an assembly of people with problems is emotionally draining–on top of the usual life concerns of marriage and raising children.

From these testimonies we see the methods of treatment God uses for healing are as varied as the situations and the personalities of those involved. Here are some prayer suggestions for clergy and their families who face heartbreaking issues every day.

- For the pastor who feels inundated by the pressures of ministry, pray the following scriptures:
  - "Not that we are competent in ourselves to claim anything for ourselves, but our competence comes from God," (2 Corinthians 3:5).
  - "Remain in me, as I also remain in you. No branch can bear fruit by itself; it must remain in the vine. Neither can you bear fruit unless you remain in me" (John 15:4)
  - "Let us not become weary in doing good, for at the proper time we will reap a harvest if we do not give up" (Galatians 6:9).
- For the church leaders, doctors, and other professionals involved in their healing, intercede with these verses:

- o "The king said to Daniel, 'Surely your God is the God of gods and the Lord of kings and a revealer of mysteries, for you were able to reveal this mystery'" (Dan. 2:47).
- o "If any of you lacks wisdom, you should ask God, who gives generously to all without finding fault, and it will be given to you" (James 1:5).
- When everything around your minister seems broken, pray these verses of joy and hope:
  - o "To him who is able to keep you from stumbling and to present you before his glorious presence without fault and with great joy" (Jude 24).
  - o "Not only so, but we also glory in our sufferings, because we know that suffering produces perseverance; perseverance, character; and character, hope. And hope does not put us to shame, because God's love has been poured out into our hearts through the Holy Spirit, who has been given to us" (Romans 5:3–5).

It can be difficult to know how to pray for such distressing issues. However, we can rely on Scripture to guide us. We are told in Romans 8:26-27 when we don't know what to pray the Spirit does two things. The Holy Spirit intercedes for us through groans (which conveys our emotions) and intercedes for us in accordance with God's will. We can be thankful in our weakness the Spirit will help us.

Pit Stop for Burnout

Restart

WINNING WISDOM

Any Church may have a mighty man of God for its pastor,
if it is willing to pay the price and that price is not a big salary,
but great praying.

R. A. TORREY

◦──◦──────────◆──────────◦──◦

Jeremy Mayfield was deemed to be an up-and-coming driver who would break into the NASCAR circuit at an early age and go on to have a long and storied career. Mayfield was named Kentucky Motor Speedway Rookie of the year in 1987, and then in 1993, Automobile Racing Club of America's (ARCA) Rookie of the Year. He won his first NASCAR Sprint Cup Series race at Pocono in 1998 and finished seventh that year in overall point standings.[199]

However, Mayfield's career stalled in May of 2009 when he tested positive for methamphetamine. He claimed he had taken Claritin-D and Adderall, both prescribed by his doctor, which caused the positive drug test. He refused to enter the NASCAR rehabilitation program and was suspended. Mayfield went to court, received a temporary injunction, and returned to driving. Days after his suspension was lifted, he tested positive again. This time he was unsuccessful in court and remains suspended to this day.

With no income and huge legal fees, Mayfield's financial problems led to eviction from his seven-bedroom, seven-bath home. Valued at $1.8 million, the 12,000-square-foot house was stripped to pay creditors.[200]

Police raided Mayfield's home in 2011 and discovered meth, plus stolen property to sustain his drug habit. In January 2014, former NASCAR driver Jeremy Mayfield was convicted of two counts of possession of drug paraphernalia and one count of possession of stolen goods in a North Carolina court. He received eighteen months of probation and was ordered to pay $88,000 in restitution to victims along with $1,100 in court costs. This plea agreement concluded a series of tragic events that haunted a racing career marked by failed drug tests and legal problems.[201]

Mayfield's tragic story mirrors some experiences in the pastorate. Though ministers usually struggle with a different set of issues, their problems can produce as much havoc and throbbing pain as Mayfield experienced.

Of 1,050 pastors surveyed by the Schaeffer Institute, every one of them—100 percent—reported a close friend or associate from seminary who had exited the ministry due to burnout, conflict in his or her church, or from a moral failure.[202] Obviously, these areas need a great deal of persevering prayer.

Burnout

"I started out pastoring with all the zeal and energy of a five-year-old on a playground, but now after over twenty years in the ministry, I honestly dread it. I used to love Sundays," posted a pastor with the initials C. E. on *PastorBurnout.com*. "Now I can't wait for them to be over." He explained that the church was dead when he first came but was now bursting at the seams with people. New buildings and money in the bank. "You would think I would be thrilled, but I'm miserable," C. E. continued online. "I spend my days dreaming about leaving and doing something else. I'm fed up with being a pastor. I know I've got it good, and I know God loves me, but I'm worn out and feel guilty to be so . . . It's not fun anymore."[203]

C. E. expresses several common symptoms of pastoral burnout. The stress of turning around a nearly dead church, exhaustion from long hours, and a lack of joy doing ministry are common characteristics. A pastor's wife from California spoke about losing sight of the calling and mission God laid out for his servant, which is another common issue. She wrote:

> "Today I woke up wondering how we got here. By here I mean a place of complete loss of direction, purpose and calling.
>
> This past year, watching my husband leave the church and return to a secular job, has been the most painful in my life. I know he says this is what he wants, though I do not believe it for a second. The depression that my husband has fallen into scares me; and I question whether or not he will pull through.
>
> Watching my husband suffer with his sadness over the loss of his ministry has been ten times

harder than any drama or problems I ever faced in the church.

I guess what I really want to say is when you have been called by God for a purpose–to not live in that purpose is to live in misery."[204]

In the 1960s, during the early days of the space program, burnout was a term used to describe rockets which propelled space capsules into the outer atmosphere of the earth. When their propellant was exhausted and their mission ended, the rockets were burned out.

These same two functions seem to signify pastoral burnout. The pastors' fuel has been emptied (physical and emotional exhaustion), and the mission concluded (spiritual indecision about direction and calling).

Brian Howard, nonprofit executive, business owner, and church planter, noticed three collapses common to leaders who burn out:

- Physical Collapses—sickness, exhaustion, insomnia, lack of energy
- Emotional Collapses—anxiety, depression
- Spiritual Collapses—spiritual discouragement, lack of spiritual interest, moral failure[205]

Burnout may seem to come out of nowhere, but it is actually a long systematic process of poor decisions or indecision. Although burnout has been studied thoroughly, the *Diagnostic and Statistical Manual of Mental Disorders* published by the American Psychiatric Association does not list burnout as a distinct disorder. Because it is so similar to depression in its symptoms and eventually leads to depression, burnout is usually treated under the large umbrella of depressive disorders by most psychiatrists, psychologists, and counselors.

Long-term stress begins the cycle and leads to a depletion of the fuel produced biochemically by our body's hormones and secreted into the brain and nervous system. These endorphins and other peptides produce an analgesic effect. When these serotonins are diminished, the body produces adrenaline to compensate.

If the stress continues—taking on additional duties, trying to meet expectations, rushing to meet fast-approaching deadlines— increasing amounts of adrenaline are produced. At this point, the body is in constant crisis mode. These high levels of epinephrine (adrenaline) in the body raise blood pressure, increase heart rate, and elevate cholesterol.

Epinephrine was designed to work in the body only in case of an emergency. If levels remain high, it is destructive to the body. Other physical problems may develop including digestive issues, insomnia, and heart disease. Emotional issues such as irritability, anxiety attacks, and depression occur as well.[206]

Pastor Wayne Cordeiro describes it this way:

> "Finally it came to a head while I was out on a run on that balmy California evening. One minute I was jogging along on the sidewalk, and the next minute I was sitting on the curb, sobbing uncontrollably. I couldn't stop, and I didn't have a clue what was happening to me.
>
> Somehow I made it through the speaking engagement that night and limped home to Hawaii. Back home again, my situation seemed to go from bad to worse. I began developing physical symptoms: erratic heartbeat, difficulty in breathing, insomnia."[207]

Cordeiro, founder and senior pastor of New Hope Christian Fellowship in Honolulu, Hawaii, exhibited both physical and emotional symptoms of burnout. Prior to his speaking engagement, he noticed ministry had changed from joy to a load that drained his energy. Even small decisions paralyzed him and his creativity waned.

Some of the same spiritual issues were also reported by this pastor from the Southwest:

> "When I first entered the ministry, I was so grateful to God for this opportunity and so full of life. [But now] my energy is gone. I was experiencing panic attacks in traffic . . . because I couldn't stand the crowd; I was becoming a prisoner in my home.
>
> What scares me is that I have no energy or excitement for this work. I sort of 'mail it in' . . . recycling old sermons . . . going through the motions. God's people should have more than that! I just don't want to do this any more . . . and that makes me feel very guilty. I prayed for years that God would allow me to go to seminary. Through many miracles, he made it possible. People still encourage me in my work. They love my sermons and Bible studies.
>
> I feel like a fake."[208]

How many times did this southwestern pastor mention directly or allude to his feelings of inadequacy, failure, and being a fake? Yet his members encouraged him and told him they enjoyed his preaching and teaching.

Rick Warren explains how dangerous feelings and emotionally based reasoning can be. "Emotional reasoning says, 'If I feel it, it must be so. If I feel like a failure, I am a failure. If I don't feel close to God, I must not be close to God. If I feel like a lousy pastor, I must be a lousy pastor.' The fact is, feelings are not always facts. Your feelings will tell you that you're helpless and hopeless, but those feelings aren't rooted in truth."[209]

No church member wants the pastor to go through burnout. The phrase "I'd rather wear out than rust out" underscores the danger.

Some pastors have struggled through this terrible experience but are now healing. Below is a prayer list to prevent your preacher from being pulverized by burnout.

Burnout Prevention Prayers

For Balance in Life

Pray for your pastor to stay balanced in all areas of his or her life. Pray based on Luke 2:52, "And Jesus grew in wisdom and stature, and in favor with God and man."

Churches are filled with people who need help, which means there will be many demands on your minister's time and energy.

Priorities. Pray for priorities to be set for (1) time for self-care, which includes body, soul, and spirit, (2) time with family, and (3) time for ministry.

Pray Matthew 6:33, "But seek first his kingdom and his righteousness, and all these things will be given to you as well."

Renewal. Pray for spiritual renewal, which could include a daily time with the Lord, an extended period of time alone with God every few months, and, after several years, a sabbatical.

Pray Hebrews 2:1, "We must pay the most careful attention, therefore, to what we have heard, so that we do not drift away."

Replenishment. Pray for emotional replenishment. Ask God to help your pastor restore the intellectual juices by reading a good book, going to a conference, or pursuing a hobby. Pray the Lord will teach him effective relational and leadership skills, as well as how to deal with conflict and criticism. Pray he will remember how to laugh.

Pray Psalm 126:2, "Our mouths were filled with laughter, our tongues with songs of joy. Then it was said among the nations, 'The LORD has done great things for them.'"

Refueling. Pray for physical refueling. Petition the Lord that your minister will schedule plenty of time for sleep, rest, and exercise. Ask God to help him or her maintain healthy eating habits and see the doctor regularly.

Pray 1 Corinthians 6:19–20, "Do you not know that your bodies are temples of the Holy Spirit, who is in you, whom you have received from God? You are not your own; you were bought at a price. Therefore honor God with your bodies."

For Healthy Boundaries

Saying No. Pray for your minister to learn to say "No" or "Later."

As Sean Fowlds points out "Ministers need to discern the difference between something that is good and something that is right. Saying no often enables us to say yes to the best God has for us."[210]

Pray Romans 12:2, "Do not conform to the pattern of this world, but be transformed by the renewing of your mind. Then you will be able to test and approve what God's will is—his good, pleasing and perfect will."

Family Time. Pray for the pastor to put family time on the calendar before ministry service. Ask God to give wisdom so all birthdays, anniversaries, and other important family events will be scheduled and guarded from interruptions.

Pray 1 Timothy 3:5, "If anyone does not know how to manage his own family, how can he take care of God's church?"

Self-Awareness. Pray your minister will serve within his or her giftings and talents. Ask God to keep the expectations of the pastor and the flock from pressing the pastor into areas they are not equipped for and don't enjoy doing.

Pray Romans 12:6, "We have different gifts, according to the grace given to each of us."

Adequate Help. Pray for your pastor to recruit help. Petition the Lord to help your minister in equipping the congregation to minister alongside each other.

Pray Ephesians 4:11–12, "So Christ himself gave the apostles, the prophets, the evangelists, the pastors and teachers, to equip his people for works of service, so that the body of Christ may be built up."

One pastor wrote, "I should have checked myself into a hospital when I started having blackouts and uncontrollable bouts of weeping. But I thought I could control it."[211] Our pastors need prayer in order to remain refreshed and vibrant for ministry.

Pit to Pulpit

When ministers were asked by Barna Research what frustrates and drains them the most, 35 percent (the highest answer) indicated: a lack of commitment among laypeople.[212]

Prayer: Pray you will commit yourself to God and pray for your pastor on a regular basis.

Scriptures: "So then, those who suffer according to God's will should commit themselves to their faithful Creator and continue to do good." *(1 Peter 4:19).*

Burnout Recovery Prayers

What about pastors who have already experienced burnout? Is there hope they can find healing to be whole persons and possibly return to ministry? Here are some intercessory prayers gleaned from clergy whose fuel tanks dropped to empty yet found healing and restoration.

Thom Rainer spoke with seventeen pastors who experienced some form of burnout but are now re-engaged and leading visionary ministries. Rainer asked each what they did to reverse their burnout. Many of the answers were similar and are reflected in these prayer requests for pastors in burnout.[213]

For Help in Recovery

Pray that pastors will get the help they need to recover from burnout. Pray that they may take the advice given to Moses in Exodus 18:14–19:

"When his father-in-law saw all that Moses was doing for the people, he said, 'What is this you are doing for the people? Why do you alone sit as judge, while all these people stand around you from morning till evening?'

Moses answered him, 'Because the people come to me to seek God's will. Whenever they have a dispute, it is brought to me, and I decide between the parties and inform them of God's decrees and instructions.'

Moses' father-in-law replied, 'What you are doing is not good. You and these people who come to you will only wear yourselves out. The work is too heavy for you; you cannot handle it alone. Listen now to me and I will give you some advice, and may God be with you.'"

A Midwestern pastor said, "One day I looked at my wife and said, 'I have a problem and I need to do something about it.' She already knew and had concerns. We talked through what I needed to do. Then I had to act on what we knew."[214]

Collaborative Effort. Pray that your pastor and church leadership will work in harmony with professionals to form a plan of restoration.

Pray Psalm 133:1, "How good and pleasant it is when God's people live together in unity!"

Kevin Conklin, a life groups pastor at Southbrook Church in Charlotte, North Carolina, wrote, "Every pastor I know has the double-edged sword of having an elder board or executive board or whatever it is called in your church. It's double-edged because on the one hand they should be there to support, encourage, and keep watch in prayer over you. But it's probably just as true that this same board may have the authority to fire you, give you a poor performance review, et cetera. So, when it comes to having to go to your board with tough personal or professional information, it can be a really hard call."[215]

Mentors. Pray for mentors or accountability partners who can see your minister through the process of restoration.

Again, recall the pattern established by Moses in Exodus 18:24–27, "Moses listened to his father-in-law and did everything he said. He chose capable men from all Israel and made them leaders of the people, officials over thousands, hundreds, fifties and tens. They served as judges for the people at all times. The difficult cases they brought to Moses, but the simple ones they decided themselves. Then Moses sent his father-in-law on his way, and Jethro returned to his own country."

Also pray James 5:16, "Therefore confess your sins to each other and pray for each other so that you may be healed."

An Australian Christian leader wrote to a fellow minister, "I have made some major internal and external changes in the way I live and think. First, I had to change my old way of thinking. For years, it didn't matter how qualified I was. I have nine years of advanced theological training, but I still felt stupid. The second change I've made in my thinking is realizing that I can't do any more than I can do, and if people don't like it that's no fault of mine. Third, nothing is that urgent."[216]

Spiritual Renewal. Pray that your pastor will renew his or her walk with the Lord.

Pray Psalm 51:10, "Create in me a pure heart, O God, and renew a steadfast spirit within me."

A Rainer survey participant admitted, "Slowly over time, I spent less and less time in the Bible and in prayer. I succumbed to the tyranny of the urgent. When I committed to reversing that pattern, my life and leadership began to renew."[217]

Time Alone with God. Intercede that your minister will spend more time in prayer and study of the Word.

Pray Isaiah 40:31, "But those who hope in the LORD will renew their strength. They will soar on wings like eagles; they will run and not grow weary, they will walk and not be faint."

Craig Groeschel, author of *Altar Ego,* said, "It's so easy to let the work of God replace your own intimacy with God. Starting with honesty about our weaknesses and vulnerabilities is vital. Through that we're able to say, I'm a Christian first—I'm a child of God first—not a pastor first. We have to fall in love with God's Word, be strengthened through prayer, have genuine Christian community where we are truly open and do life with others. Sometimes as pastors we let those life-changing basics slip."[218]

Renewed Vision for Ministry. Pray your leader will recapture his or her vision for ministry.

Pray Proverbs 29:18, "Where there is no vision, the people are unrestrained, But happy is he who keeps the law" (NASB).

"When I first arrived at this church, I had great visions and excitement," explained a Rainer participant. "But I got caught up in negativity and trivial things, and I lost my vision. But recently I asked

God to restore my dream and vision for my church, and He's already answering that prayer."[219]

Passion for Evangelism. Pray that your minister will see a world that needs Christ.

Pray Matthew 9:36, "When he saw the crowds, he had compassion on them, because they were harassed and helpless, like sheep without a shepherd."

"I got so busy doing church that I started neglecting engaging people in the world," said another pastor in Rainer's group. "Burnout can be the result of looking inwardly too much. I asked God to give me a greater vision for our church's community."[220]

A Servant's Heart. Petition God for your pastor to re-cultivate a servant's heart.

Pray John13:14, "Now that I, your Lord and Teacher, have washed your feet, you also should wash one another's feet."

Kyle Idleman, author of *Gods at War*, said, "Insecurity for me isn't as much about how I perceive people viewing me, my personal insecurity comes more from my own view of me. A few years ago, I was really struggling with this. I ended up going into the garage, grabbing a can of black spray paint, and painting the classic words from the Apostle Paul on my closet wall: I DIE DAILY. For me, every time I saw my indoor graffiti, it summed up my challenge."[221]

Another minister said, "I had trouble admitting that I had an ego problem. I always wanted things my way. God got to me and showed me that my calling in life is to serve others. It is absolutely amazing to see my leadership passion restored as I put myself last to the needs of others."[222]

For Emotional Healing

Pray that your leader will heal emotionally and be re-energized.

Pray Hebrews 6:19, "We have this hope as an anchor for the soul, firm and secure."

An Australian minister wrote, "What gave me the most hope during my season of wrestling with burnout was my wife. Also, my children and my support network kept reinforcing, 'You will get better.' The night I experienced my meltdown I felt the Lord speak to me from Psalm 41:3. [The LORD sustains them on their sickbed and restores them from their bed of illness.] I declare that Scripture every night."[223]

Freedom from Comparisons. Intercede that your pastor will avoid comparison to other pastors, comparison to other churches, and worrying what others think.

Pray Galatians 1:10, "Am I now trying to win the approval of human beings, or of God? Or am I trying to please people? If I were still trying to please people, I would not be a servant of Christ."

"One of the most freeing things of my ministry was to stop comparing myself to other pastors, and my church to other churches. I finally got it that God doesn't love pastors of larger churches more than He loves me," said one enlightened survey participant.[224]

Megachurch pastor Craig Groeschel relates, "To be honest, it's not easy to overcome people-pleasing and focus solely on what God thinks. Social media can get to me, so one thing I do is avoid social media during ministry times. A disciplined life of prayer helps me keep my eyes on Christ and off of the approval of people."[225]

A Positive Attitude. Ask God to help your minister change his or her attitude from negative to positive.

Pray Proverbs 11:25, "Whoever refreshes others will be refreshed"

And Romans 15:5–6, "May the God who gives endurance and encouragement give you the same attitude of mind toward each other that Christ Jesus had, so that with one mind and one voice you may glorify the God and Father of our Lord Jesus Christ."

"I don't know why I let the critics dominate my time and thoughts. When I stopped letting them control me, and when I started spending more time with positive and great people in the church," explained one senior pastor in a questionnaire "my entire emotional state improved dramatically."[226]

Wayne Cordeiro stated, "My first step toward rehabilitation was to see my depression as a positive challenge that drew me closer to Christ on a daily basis."[227]

Joy and Gratitude. Pray your spiritual leader will find joy again by celebrating and rejoicing more, expressing gratitude, and having more fun with friends.

Pray Psalm 118:24, "This is the day which the LORD has made; Let us rejoice and be glad in it" (NASB).

And 1 Thessalonians 5:18, "Give thanks in all circumstances; for this is God's will for you in Christ Jesus."

From the Rainer survey, "I realized that there is a difference between taking my ministry seriously and taking myself too seriously. I have learned to lighten up and laugh more. As a result, I find myself rejoicing in the Lord more."[228]

A minister on the East Coast commented, "I have learned that I need replenishing friends who are safe. I make sure that I have those kinds of friends."[229]

Another church leader told Rainer, "One of the ways I dealt with my impending burnout was to commit to handwrite five letters of gratitude a week. It was amazing to see how my vision began to restore when I took the focus off me and expressed gratitude to others."[230]

Avoiding Emotional Drains. Pray your pastor will terminate relationships or activities that empty his or her gas tank, and will seek activities that energize.

Pray Ephesians 4:11–12, "So Christ himself gave the apostles, the prophets, the evangelists, the pastors and teachers, to equip his people for works of service, so that the body of Christ may be built up."

One senior pastor told Rainer, "There was this church member that made an appointment with me almost every week. He was so negative and so draining of my emotional energy. I knew he had his own emotional problems, but I knew I wasn't equipped to deal with them. When I finally got the courage to end our counseling relationship and refer him to a professional, I felt like a weight had been lifted off me."[231]

Another reported, "I tend to be a prideful person, so I don't like to admit that I am not very good at something. Well, I'm a poor administrator, so administrative work drains me. When I finally got the courage to admit I wasn't very good at it, I had a lay volunteer step right in and take much of the work off me."[232]

Tool Box

For the seventh time in his career Jimmie Johnson won in April 2017 at Texas Motor Speedway. But it didn't come easy for the accomplished triathlete. The heat and wind made Johnson's left side cramp up as he slipped past Joey Logano near the end of the race. After a burnout and Victory Lane celebrations, he went to the infield care center where he received three bags of intravenous fluids. He told the media his drink system didn't work from the beginning of the race.[233]

Prayer: Pray your pastor will be refreshed after large projects or programs are completed.

Scriptures: "The king [David] and all the people with him arrived at their destination exhausted. And there he refreshed himself." *(2 Samuel 16:14).*

Pray for Rest

Ask God to guide your preacher to realize the many roads to burnout, but they all lead to the same destination: exhaustion. Pray that your pastor can recover from the lament expressed in Jeremiah 45:3, "I am worn out with groaning and find no rest."

Julie Pierce, who ministers to women through her coaching, speaking, and writing, said, "I was overworked, over-caffeinated, overcommitted, and overwhelmed. I felt depleted in every way possible. And eventually, I found myself infected from head to toe with a widespread epidemic: exhaustion. I had the burnout bug"[234]

Physical Rest. Pray for your pastor to rest his or her body. After Elijah demonstrated the power of God at Mount Carmel, he instructed the people to seize and kill the prophets of Baal. Jezebel threatened to do the same to Elijah. He ran for his life and finally collapsed under a bush, exhausted from his running.

Elijah's story is recorded in 1 Kings 18:16–19:3. At one point, Elijah cried out to God: "'I have had enough, LORD,' he said. 'Take my life; I am no better than my ancestors.' Then he lay down under the bush and fell asleep (19:4–5).

"All at once an angel touched him and said, 'Get up and eat.' He looked around, and there by his head was some bread baked over hot coals, and a jar of water. He ate and drank and then lay down again'" (19:5–6).

Julie Pierce recalled, "At the end of every day, I would collapse into my bed and pray for a few hours of sleep, only to find my mind so wound up that sleep wouldn't come. When the alarm went off the next morning, I would force myself out of bed, dreading the demands of the day."[235]

Wayne Cordeiro states, "We are never more vulnerable to depression than when we are totally fatigued or overtired. One of the very first steps in reversing depression and regaining a sense of resilience is rest. Increase your rest until you begin to feel some semblance of renewal, even if it begins with small doses."[236]

Calendar Control. Ask God to help your minister schedule rest into his or her calendar.

Pray Matthew 11:28–30, "Come to me, all you who are weary and burdened, and I will give you rest. Take my yoke upon you and learn from me, for I am gentle and humble in heart, and you will find rest for your souls. For my yoke is easy and my burden is light."

Also pray Leviticus 23:31–32, "You shall do no work at all. This is to be a lasting ordinance for the generations to come, wherever you live. It is a day of sabbath rest for you."

"Schedule rests before your calendar fills up," remarked Wayne Cordeiro, based on his experience. "Rest is not an afterthought; it has to be a primary responsibility. It brings a rhythm back to life and a cadence that makes life sustainable. If you are tired, your soul gets weary. And if your soul gets weary, you've depleted more than you can afford."[237]

Andrew McMillan, pastor of Christian Community of Faith in Medellin, Columbia, said, "My church knows that I take Mondays off, and Tuesday is my prayer day. I tell them if the church is on fire, call the fire department."[238]

Proper Diet and Exercise. Intercede that your clergy will get exercise regularly, eat healthy foods, and follow doctor's orders.

Pray 1 Corinthians 6:19–20, "Do you not know that your bodies are temples of the Holy Spirit, who is in you, whom you have received from God? You are not your own; you were bought at a price. Therefore honor God with your bodies."

And pray Ephesians 5:29, "After all, no one ever hated their own body, but they feed and care for their body, just as Christ does the church."

A Rainer survey participant said, "In my busyness, I started eating more, exercising less, and sleeping fitfully. I stayed tired and depressed. But when I got into an exercise routine and ate better, my whole outlook changed."[239]

Pastor Ron Edmondson said, "I discovered that my running time—or when I exercise—is one of the few times each day where I am not answering emails, taking phone calls or doing something that requires mental power. I am better able to maintain my weight . . . I feel better. I sleep better. My blood pressure tests lower. . . My best ideas come while I am running. I suppose because my body is energized and I'm free from other distractions, I'm so creative while I'm running. Some of my deepest, most intimate times with God come when I'm on a long run. I find if I'm especially stressed, a good sweat gives me a calmer perspective. It's an excellent way to decompress."[240]

Family Wholeness. One final area of prayer for those who are headed into or are in burnout is the pastor's family. Sometimes the demands of ministry spill over on the spouse and children. The family becomes overwhelmed with responsibilities and commitments, because they pitch in to help with the burden of the burned-out pastor. Often the spouse and kids are equally exhausted and possibly even on the edge of burnout themselves.

"Burnout is a very real issue in ministry," blogged youth pastor's wife Miranda Vande Kuyt. "As a pastor's wife, mother, and self-employed consultant, I have struggled with trying to do too many things for too many people on my own strength for far too long."

She received help by attending a Shaunti Feldhahn seminar about juggling life for the modern Christian woman.[241]

Erin Wheeler, senior pastor's wife at University Baptist Church in Fayetteville, Arkansas, wrote, "We've all had those days. You know, the ones where you crawl into bed, makeup still on, wondering if it's okay not to brush your teeth just this once. All the while, you wonder what actually happened to the minutes that evaporated into history."[242]

After her husband hit an emotional wall caused by burnout, this pastor's wife said, "My husband trusted me more than anyone else on our staff so he found it easy to ask me to take on new ministries. The more I accomplished the more people (including my husband) admired me. But it took a toll. I didn't realize how tired and burned out I was until we retired. Then I emotionally collapsed. It took two years for me to even consider volunteering for anything at all. I didn't even want to attend any kind of women's events, let alone help with them."[243]

For forty years the children of Israel meandered in an arid area looking for sustenance. Ministry families in burnout or at high risk for burnout can relate to the Israelites. Both lost sight of their purpose and felt as if they were going in circles.

For the family members in burnout, please pray the words God gave the children of Israel in Deuteronomy 8:1-3.

"Be careful to follow every command I am giving you today, so that you may live and increase and may enter and possess the land the Lord promised on oath to your ancestors.

Remember how the Lord your God led you all the way in the wilderness these forty years, to humble and test you in order to know what was in your heart, whether or not you would keep his commands.

He humbled you, causing you to hunger and then feeding you with manna, which neither you nor your ancestors had known, to teach you that man does not live on bread alone but on every word that comes from the mouth of the Lord."

The Unbusy Warrior

You may ask, "How can I possibly pray on a regular basis for my pastor? I know it is important, but I don't have the time."

The Lord revealed how my commitment and priorities were lacking. To develop a richer prayer life; I needed an uncluttered life, constant communion with the Lord, and a consecrated life. I made a concentrated effort to clear the chaos and center my life on his Word.

Will you join me in this quest to free ourselves from the mess of everyday life and devote ourselves to a specific time of prayer each day? Then as we go about our days, we will maintain a mental solitude, which reaches back to our prayer time and breathes a continual presence with our Lord.

In his book *Prayer*, Richard Foster writes: "At first we thought solitude was a way to recharge our batteries in order to enter life's many competitions with new vigor and strength. In time, however; we find that solitude gives us power not to win the rat race but to ignore the rat race altogether. Slowly, we find ourselves letting go of our inner compulsions to acquire more wealth than we need, look more youthful than we are, attain more status than is wise. In the stillness, our false, busy selves are unmasked and seen for the impostors they truly are."[244]

We live in a busy, performance-oriented world. The responsibility of minister and intercessor alike remains - to seek God's purposes and priorities for our lives. As prayer warriors, we need to guard our schedules so we have time to pray and help our minsters find their niches in kingdom work. We love our pastors so we must pray burnout does not take them out of the race.

10

The Pain of Moral Issues and Forced Exits

Trading Paint

WINNING WISDOM

May God help me, if you cease to pray for me!
Let me know the day, and I must cease to preach.

CHARLES H. SPURGEON

Aaron Fike, born in Galesburg, Illinois, began his racing in 2001 in the USAC Silver Crown Series. He became the youngest driver to win a Silver Crown race. When he finished tenth in points for the season, his efforts earned him the Rookie of the Year award. The winning continued in 2002 and 2003, when he won seven midget feature races as well as the Badger Midget Auto Racing Association championship.

Fike began racing in NASCAR part-time in 2004, for GIC-Mixon Motorsports. He continued racing in NASCAR during the 2005–2006 season. In 2007 he competed in the Craftsman Truck Series. Driving for Red Horse Racing, Fike experienced great success his first year in Craftsman, with four top-ten finishes.

He was in the running for Rookie of the Year, but it all faded when he and his fiancée, Cassandra "Casi" Davidson, a crew member for Red Horse Racing, were arrested in the parking lot of an amusement park. Both were charged with possession of heroin and drug paraphernalia. Four days later, both were suspended indefinitely by NASCAR.[245]

Tom DeLoach, owner and general manager of Red Horse Racing, said, "We had no idea what Fike was going through. Not those of us who worked beside him every weekend or, to the best of my knowledge, any of the people we raced against every weekend."[246]

In 2008, Fike admitted to ESPN Sports he suffered for six years with a dependency on painkillers before resorting to once-a-week recreational use of heroin, which continued for eight months. Several weeks before his arrest, Fike's heroin use turned into a daily habit, including race days.[247] After spending four months in treatment, he stated that his habit almost killed him at least once. He believes the arrest saved his and Casi's lives.

Fike's situation caused NASCAR to rethink its drug testing policy. Prior to Fike's arrest, drug testing of drivers and crew was only required when based on reasonable suspicion of abuse. Because Fike had been able to drive without detection, the NASCAR policy was changed to a system of random testing in 2009.

"I was able to race with it in my system," Fike said. He hopes his story will save others' lives. After drug rehab, two years of probation that included weekly drug testing, and the establishment of a nonprofit group called Racing Against Drugs, Fike started racing again in midget cars.[248]

Clergy, like NASCAR personnel, are all part of the human race. Every one of us are flawed people who slip into trouble from time to time. Sometimes these problems erupt into serious messes that affect family members, coworkers, and the community.

Some ministers unknowingly stumble into a pitfall. Others flirt with danger. All of us, including pastors, are only one decision away from sin.

Moral Issues

Pastors experiencing burnout sometimes resort to alcohol, drugs, smoking, or overeating to deaden the pain and bring some relief. The depression that accompanies burnout often leads to a decrease in libido. The burned-out pastor may be disinterested in his or her spouse and vulnerable to pornography and affairs.

Yet burnout is only one of many factors that can lead to a moral failure. Let's look at some cases of moral failure among clergy and identify ways to pray for pastors who may be facing temptation. We'll begin with pastors who realized they were on a dangerous path and reported their own behavior.

Confessed

Before serving as a Methodist minister for eleven years, John Eades spent twenty years as a therapist counseling drug and alcohol addicts. However, his expertise in compulsive behavior did not avert his own descent into gambling.

Some friends hounded Eades into going to a casino with them. Although he had never gambled before, the urge to play the slots soon led to daily visits.

"I went every afternoon after work and stayed until late, and I'd go every weekend," said Eades.

Over the course of two years, he maxed out seventeen credit cards and accumulated $245,000 in debts. One night on his way home from gambling, Eades pulled into a rest stop. He had decided to end it all.

He opened his glove compartment to grab his .357 magnum, but it was not there. Upon returning home, Eades hugged his wife and thanked her for hiding his gun and saving his life.

"I didn't take the gun to save your life," she told him. "I sold it so we could pay the electric bill."

Now in recovery, Eades is amazed at the power the addiction wielded over his life. "It's just like you were an insane person," said Eades. "You cannot believe the things you did."

He further believes recovery is impossible without God's intervention, and he recognizes the vital role his wife plays in his recovery.

"It's very important to have a wife who loves you enough to stay with you through it," Eades said.[249]

—— • ——

Richard Yasinski planted a coffeehouse church in Springfield, Missouri. Even after four years it had not grown beyond a few dozen teenagers with tattoos and piercings. Compared to other pastors his age, Yasinski felt like a failure. He became depressed.

Medical issues furthered his problems. After colon surgery, his doctor prescribed a narcotic for pain. Yasinski paid little attention to the warning label: "This drug should not be taken by those susceptible to alcohol addiction."

He drank heavily in high school, and his parents were alcoholics. But at age eighteen, Yasinski had received Jesus and was delivered from alcohol. Now, years later, his depression plus his pain medication combined into a chemical reaction he had not experienced since his teens.

On a frigid day as he shoveled snow, Yasinski remembered drinking a half pint of brandy more than twenty years before. *What a great way to warm up and relax*, he thought. *Just once wouldn't hurt.*

It wasn't just once. Yasinki's drinking turned into months of repeated episodes. Within six months, his habit grew to a bottle or more of brandy every day. He hid bottles behind the water heater in the garage, in the attic, and in the toilet tank.

Yasinski kept his secret from everyone, including his wife. "I felt like I could not tell a soul. No one would understand. I felt so guilty, but I couldn't stop."

After a year of addiction, he revealed his problem to his wife, then to an elder. Unable to cope any longer and while hungover, Yasinski called a meeting of key church leaders, confessed his dependence on alcohol, and announced his resignation.

However, the leadership rejected his resignation. They vowed to work with him through his crisis and promised his job would be held as long as necessary.

"Instead of kicking me to the curb, they showed nothing but grace." Yasinski spent the next forty days in a Christian rehabilitation center in Florida.

Years later the coffeehouse was renamed Center City Church and relocated to an area laden with homelessness, drug abuse, and alcoholism. The church is home to dozens of recovering addicts.

"What I went through gives me validity in their eyes. If I had been allowed to resign, I would be in prison or dead," said Yasinski.[250]

—•—

Luke Gilkerson, a campus pastor for six years, feels his addiction to pornography paralleled the same lunacy the Israelites displayed. They wanted to return to slavery in Egypt.

"Yes, in my sober moments, I could see the ugliness of porn for what it was. But there were many times I rushed back to porn like a dog to its vomit," he said, alluding to Proverbs 26:11.

"Something in me *wanted* to be addicted, wanted the slavery. . . For me, it wasn't that slavery to porn was all that desirable, but it was easier for me than trusting God. In order to finally overcome my addiction to porn, I needed to confess my sin of unbelief."

When Gilkerson felt inadequate and rejected, he turned to porn, to the fantasy world that provided a temporary illusion of intimacy.

At times, he became angry at God for not giving him the wife he so "deserved" and the life he desperately longed for. He recognized God knew him better than he knew himself. "He knows exactly what blessings are best for me in His perfect timing."

Finally, Gilkerson realized, "The only thing that cures a longing for Egypt is a longing for the Promised Land. I needed to believe what God offers me is far better than the false promises of porn." Gilkerson now serves as the general editor and primary author of the Covenant Eyes blog.[251]

—•—

Paul Foster served as a bivocational pastor in a remote area of southeast Alaska. Foster slipped into a depression caused by his feelings of inadequacy. He was not able to grow his church beyond one hundred members. His situation worsened when some medical issues cropped up.

While exercising, Foster experienced a sharp pain in his lower back. A doctor prescribed a narcotic. Foster soon realized the medication helped him cope with life's other pains as well.

"When I first took a pill or two, it would give me a buzz so I could converse with people like I normally couldn't," said Foster. "I was connecting with people like never before. I began to take pills based on planned social interactions."

Foster now serves as program coordinator at Testimony Life Resources, an addictions counseling ministry in California. "So often we're afraid to tell people what we've been through and what God has done in our lives. We just need to share a portion of our story to let others know they're not the only ones struggling."

He feels many pastors do not know where to turn for help. "People don't think pastors are supposed to have these problems, and they don't feel safe in sharing problems because they can lose their jobs."[252]

———•———

"I thought it was innocent at the time."

"She was a church staff member, so we spent a lot of time together. She'd sit in my office, and we'd talk. At times she told me about the difficulties in her marriage, and I counseled her. But I should have stopped her right there," said the associate pastor. "I was filling a need I had no right to fill."

Although the pastor and staff member never embraced or touched, their emotional attraction had a fun vibe. He had a great wife and family, yet he often thought of this staff member.

One day while he was on the phone, she came up behind him and pinched his buttock. Fear kicked in, and he blew the whistle on himself. He confessed his unfaithful thoughts to his senior pastor, then to his wife. Next, he became accountable to a few selected, trusted people. He also asked his wife to watch out for danger signs.

"What's really scary? I had a good marriage, and I was *still* vulnerable. Imagine what might happen if someone's in a bad marriage! It all came down to me being stupid and making a stupid choice, of enjoying sin and flirting with it."[253]

Prayers for Prevention

Do these five testimonies break your heart? Did you have to stop reading to shed tears of sorrow? Would you like for your church to take action so your pastor will not be sifted like wheat (see Luke 22:31)? Pray that your pastor will insist on the following accountability in his and his coworkers lives.

Accountability Software. Let's all pray our church leadership will see the wisdom of requiring and installing accountability software on staff computers, laptops, tablets, and mobile phones in the office and at home.

Pray in the spirit of Matthew 5:28, "But I tell you that anyone who looks at a woman lustfully has already committed adultery with her in his heart."

Opposite-Sex and Child Protection Policies. Pray for written church policies regarding counseling someone of the opposite sex, polices concerning visitation, and policies of not being alone with a child.

Pray 1 Corinthians 10:13, "No temptation has overtaken you except what is common to mankind. And God is faithful; he will not let you be tempted beyond what you can bear. But when you are tempted, he will also provide a way out so that you can endure it."

Financial Policies. Ask God to guide the leadership in setting up sound financial practices and ordering regular audits.

Pray Hebrews 4:13, "Nothing in all creation is hidden from God's sight. Everything is uncovered and laid bare before the eyes of him to whom we must give account."

Accountability Partnerships. Intercede that the pastor will find at least two accountability partners, see a Christian counselor, or get involved in a support group.

Pray Ecclesiastes 4:12, "Though one may be overpowered, two can defend themselves. A cord of three strands is not quickly broken."

Although these prayers will set up boundaries of protection for our pastors, they will not eliminate the possibility of transgression. Satan has tricked people into wrongdoing since the Garden of Eden. If our minister admits to a transgression, we must pray for his or her healing and restoration.

Caught

In the previous five scenarios, the ministers felt convicted, confessed their sins, and started plans of restoration. But some pastors can not seem to bring themselves to confide in someone and ask for help. Sometimes this is because they feel ashamed or because they fear getting fired and experiencing the financial consequences that will follow. Most clergy have little or no training outside of theology, so they fear it will be difficult to obtain other employment.

Derek Rishmawy, the director of college and young adult ministries at Trinity United Presbyterian Church in Orange County, California, said:

> "The fear of marital or ministry failure has haunted me ever since I enrolled in seminary. I'm a church kid, so I've seen the carnage this sort of thing wreaks, even when you're not a nationally recognized name. Your family, your church, and your

local community feel the effects, and that's enough. The reality is, because of indwelling sin, I *could* do that. Maybe not easily. Maybe not the exact same sin. But we're fools to forget what the Lord said to Cain 'Sin is crouching at your door, it desires to have you'" (Genesis 4:7).[254]

Sadly some improper actions by pastors go on for so long or become so awful they come to the attention of those outside their church. In some cases, law enforcement and the media may become involved. Actions by church leaders who try to remedy the problem may also become public.

The following are cases involving ministers who were caught in wrongdoing:

— • —

Kendall Freeman started viewing pornography at age nine by sneaking peeks at pornographic magazines under the counter of a drugstore. His habit continued off and on through Bible college and into full-time ministry.

When his wife noticed 900 numbers on the family phone bill, he deflected the blame. "I let her fight the phone company for me over some $400 bill," Freeman said.

Later, his visits to porn sites brought a virus into the church computer system. When his computer was discovered as the culprit, a coworker suggested it might have been students who accessed his computer while it was unlocked.

Freeman went along with the idea. A student minister for twelve years, he said, "So I let the students, these students I loved, take the fall for it."

After that incident, the church continued to monitor Internet usage. One day a veteran pastor came to Freeman's office with a list of vulgar websites he had frequented that morning.

When his wife learned he had been fired for viewing porn on his church computer, she kicked him out of the house.

Later they went to a park to begin working on the problem. The next Sunday, Freeman confessed his porn problem to the church at all three services. "I loved the people at Westerville, and they deserved more than me just walking away," he said.

His wife said the push to confess came from God "When we confess, what stone can Satan throw at [us]? There's nothing to hide anymore." They attended a week-long intensive course at a Georgia church that taught them how to engage in spiritual warfare.

Three years later, Freeman and his wife say their marriage is better than ever. They still attend the same church where he served as student pastor. He now "yearns to minister to ministers."[255]

Pornography has been a problem in our society for decades. Due to easy accessibility via the internet, porn consumption has exploded like a supernova. In a 2015 study, 15 percent of Christian women and 64 percent of Christian men (compared to 30 percent of non-Christian women and 65 percent of non-Christian men) reported they viewed pornography at least once a month. Further, 75 percent of pastors admitted they did not make themselves accountable to anyone for their Internet use.[256]

—•—

"It was a warm spring day, but I was depressed beyond depressed. It is difficult to describe how empty I felt. I was cycling in the shadows again—lapsing into lust and compulsive sexual behavior."[257]

Husband, father, and pastor, T. C. Ryan, had not used Internet pornography since installing a software monitoring program on his computer. But even while being treated with antidepressants, he was so despondent he resorted to default behaviors. He went to a park where men sometimes gathered to swap porn. He met someone there and bought a magazine.

"God in heaven," Ryan prayed, "I cannot believe after everything I've done and all the grace you've shown me, I'm here in this place, just cycling and cycling and cycling. I don't care what you do with me, but you have to do something. Please."

As he walked back to his car, a police officer pulled up. Ryan was questioned about his activities in the park. The officer arrested him and charged him with a misdemeanor for lewd and lascivious behavior.

Ryan spent twenty-six hours in jail. At the time, he said, "My life was over."[258]

Ryan went to his wife, the mother of their four children, and told her he wanted to go into counseling. She heartily agreed. With the help of a counselor, he began to realize how much pain his depression and anger had caused his family. His counselor walked him through the scars of his childhood abuse, the coping mechanism of dissociation that had resulted, and how to understand the triggers in his life that set him up for failure. Ryan, who now speaks, pastors, and leads retreats, authored the book *Ashamed No More*.

Pit to Pulpit

H. B. London Jr. wrote, "One day, one of our secretaries in Pastoral Ministries mentioned to me that she had received five calls that morning from pastors on the issue of pornography. Initially, I thought the callers were looking for counseling aids, but I soon discovered that they themselves were hooked. One had been struggling with the temptations for more than twenty years."[259]

Prayer: Pray your minister will avoid pornography.

Scripture: "Do not be wise in your own eyes; fear the LORD and shun evil" *(Proverbs 3:7).*

A Kansas pastor was charged in 2013 with writing more than $10,000 in bad checks. Leavenworth County Attorney Todd Thompson told the media, "Realtors and property management services started realizing he was hitting all of their facilities. They came together and said something needed to be done."

Pastor Jimmie Hancock started the rental process by writing a check under his church's name. When the check bounced, he blamed his church. Hancock would receive several months of residency before the eviction was served.

"These people all trusted him because of his vocation and I think that's why he was able to sustain it for so long," said the county attorney.

Hancock pled guilty to three felony counts of passing worthless checks. The judge ordered him to repay the money.[260]

———— • ————

Christi Gibson found her husband's body at their on-campus home. Pastor John Gibson committed suicide just six days after the Ashley Madison list was posted. Gibson, a pastor and professor at New Orleans Baptist Theological Seminary, left a suicide note detailing his demons and depression.

He stated that his name was on the list and said he was, "Very, very, very sorry." Gibson left behind a wife, son, and daughter.

"It was a moment that life doesn't prepare you for," said Christi Gibson. "I had to call my kids. How do you tell your kids that their dad is gone and that he took his own life?"[261]

Ashley Madison is a website that promises to match users, for a fee, with someone who wants to have an affair. The site's motto is, "Life Is Short. Have an Affair."

The site received global attention when hackers stole its customer data on July 15, 2015, and threatened to post the data online if the Ashley Madison site was not shut down. A few names were released later in July. When the site remained active, the hackers released customer data on August 18, including thirty-two million names along with email and physical addresses, credit card numbers, and sexual preferences.[262, 263]

Ed Stetzer, an expert on ecclesiology and missions, reacted to the Ashley Madison motto with "Life Is Eternal. Don't Have an Affair."

Based on his conversations with leaders from several denominations, Stetzer estimates at least 400 church leaders were on the cheater's website.[264]

—— • ——

Shelly Duffer received a call from the local sheriff's department, asking her to come to the station. She could not believe what she was hearing and hung up on the officer. He couldn't possibly be questioning her husband about an inappropriate relationship with a girl in their congregation.

Duffer then called the church but could not reach her husband. She called the senior pastor's wife, who said she would be right over. They went to the sheriff's department together. The account Shelly's husband had given the officers was, in her words, "Nightmarish."

The next morning, Duffer's husband was arrested and charged. A second victim came forward four days later. It became a high-profile case. Eventually Duffer was charged with eighteen felony counts, which resulted in a conviction and a sentence of seventeen years in prison.

"How do you explain to your children (ages 8, 9, 13, 15) that their daddy has committed sex crimes?" Shelly asked, "Our lives had been shattered by monstrous sin."[265]

—•—

The 160 members of Shiloh Missionary Baptist Church offered compassion and prayers when Reverend Juan Demetrius McFarland revealed he was HIV-positive and had been diagnosed with full-blown AIDS. The minister of twenty-three years was later terminated when leadership found he knowingly had sex with members in the church building *after* his diagnosis and without revealing his medical status to the women involved. The Montgomery, Alabama, church leaders also confirmed, "McFarland admitted to drug use and receiving funds for business trips he never took."

One stunned church member said, "Who does this to people and you are the leader? Who does this?"

Another said, "The fact that he didn't tell them [about his AIDS diagnosis] at all, that's a crime in itself."

"I believe that he should be put on trial," said still another member.

Deacon Nathan Williams Jr. said, "Our moves are going to come directly from counsel. We want peace and we want to do things right, legally. We are not looking to hurt him. We are looking to get the church back."[266]

Prayers of Healing and Restoration

Confession. Pray the pastor will get right with God, will confess to his or her spouse and family (if the children are of appropriate age), and will confess to church leaders and assume full responsibility for his or her actions.

Pray Psalm 38:18, "I confess my iniquity; I am troubled by my sin"

And 1 John 1:9, "If we confess our sins, he is faithful and just and will forgive us our sins and purify us from all unrighteousness."

"God does not intend for us to be alone," said Darrell Brazell, pastor and director of recovery ministries for New Hope Fellowship in Lawrence, Kansas. "The most important thing I did to start walking in freedom was the very thing I was most terrified to do—tell others the truth about my struggle. Sin, especially sexual bondage, is too powerful to fight through alone. We find our way to freedom when we start being honest with others."[267]

Care for Victims. Intercede for those who have been hurt, betrayed, or victimized. If there are victims, ask God to lead the church board to care for and provide safety for them.

Pray Psalm 78:72, "And David shepherded them with integrity of heart; with skillful hands he led them"

Also pray Acts 20:28, "Keep watch over yourselves and all the flock of which the Holy Spirit has made you overseers. Be shepherds of the church of God, which he bought with his own blood."

"Despite the fact that this situation [sexual misconduct] happens far too often, 'Pastoring Your Church through Trauma' is not a class taught in many seminaries or church growth conferences," said Dorothy Greco, wife of a church leader.[268]

In the wake of a clergy failure, another minister's wife said, "Care was given to the victims and the grieving, confused teens. We re-examined policies to better protect the youth."[269]

Grace-Filled Communication. Pray for your church leadership as they formulate a plan of communication, healing, and restoration for your minister and your church. Pray they will balance grace and truth.

Pray James 1:5, "If any of you lacks wisdom, you should ask God, who gives generously to all without finding fault, and it will be given to you"

Also pray 1 Kings 4:29, "God gave Solomon wisdom and very great insight, and a breadth of understanding as measureless as the sand on the seashore"

Galatians 6:1, "Brothers and sisters, if someone is caught in a sin, you who live by the Spirit should restore that person gently. But watch yourselves, or you also may be tempted."

"When our senior pastor had his affair, the regional overseer came and met with the staff and leaders for several days," said Dorothy Greco.[270]

Adult Bible study teacher Darrel Rowland reports, "There are two extremes: one set of fallen leaders who seemingly are too quickly restored to their positions, and another who effectively have been left to rot as if they have committed the unpardonable sin."[271]

Protection from Gossip. Ask God to protect your church from gossip.

Pray Proverbs 16:28, "A perverse person stirs up conflict, and a gossip separates close friends"

Also pray 2 Corinthians 12:20, "For I am afraid that when I come I may not find you as I want you to be, and you may not find me as you want me to be. I fear that there may be discord, jealousy, fits of rage, selfish ambition, slander, gossip, arrogance and disorder."

One website for church leaders offers this advice: "Shut down gossip whenever and wherever you hear it. Create a culture where talking about other's failures is odd and unacceptable."[272]

Submission to Authority. Pray that the minister will submit to the plan laid out by leadership.

Pray Hebrews 13:17, "Have confidence in your leaders and submit to their authority, because they keep watch over you as those who must give an account. Do this so that their work will be a joy, not a burden, for that would be of no benefit to you."

Ed Stetzer wrote, "Cast everything on him. It isn't possible for you to know what will happen next, so you must trust him implicitly. You will need to confess, and when you do, you are taking a risk. It may very well get worse before it gets better, but none of it will catch God by surprise. Now is the time to commit yourself to his purposes whatever they may be."[273]

A Gracious Response. When confession is made, pray that the assembly and leaders will respond with forgiveness, not anger and judgment.

Pray Colossians 3:13, "Bear with each other and forgive one another if any of you has a grievance against someone. Forgive as the Lord forgave you"

And Psalm 130:3–4, "If you, LORD, kept a record of sins, Lord, who could stand? But with you there is forgiveness, so that we can, with reverence, serve you."

The wife of a leadership team member offered this advice: "When a leader teaches on the importance of upholding a biblical lifestyle and then lives duplicitously, it's no surprise that we would feel angry at the hypocrisy and deceit—but bitterness is not inevitable. We can prevent it from taking root if we validate the anger (versus minimizing or dismissing it), offer a safe context for people to process, and then encourage them to work toward forgiveness, understanding that it's a process—and sometimes a lengthy one."[274]

Courage During Restoration. Ask God to give strength and courage to the pastor and those holding him or her accountable to work through the entire process.

Pray Galatians 6:9, "Let us not become weary in doing good, for at the proper time we will reap a harvest if we do not give up"

Also Ephesians 4:2, "Be completely humble and gentle; be patient, bearing with one another in love"

And Romans 12:10, "Be devoted to one another in love."

Paul Boatman, dean of Lincoln Christian Seminary and professor of pastoral care and counseling, said, "Those instances in which I have seen a 'fallen leader' responsibly reengage have *always* included intense accountability relationships."[275]

Full Restoration. Pray there will be celebration as steps are completed in healing and restoration.

Pray 2 Corinthians 13:11, "Finally, brothers and sisters, rejoice! Strive for full restoration, encourage one another, be of one mind, live in peace. And the God of love and peace will be with you"

Psalm 126:5, "Those who sow with tears will reap with songs of joy."

An anonymous minister's spouse said, "Trust that your mourning will one day become dancing."[276]

Victory over Disillusionment. Petition God to help members help each other through their pain and disillusionment.

Pray Hebrews 10:23–25, "Let us hold unswervingly to the hope we profess, for he who promised is faithful. And let us consider how we may spur one another on toward love and good deeds, not giving up meeting together, as some are in the habit of doing, but encouraging one another—and all the more as you see the Day approaching."

A church leader's spouse said, "Young believers or individuals who hold unrealistic expectations for their leaders are particularly susceptible to disillusionment. Thoughtful, caring conversations will serve to not only help them understand their disappointment but also set more realistic expectations in the future."[277]

Growth in the Body. Praise God for the hidden blessings in the process, such as others also confessing their secret sins and the entire congregation drawing closer together.

Pray Ezra 10:1, "While Ezra was praying and confessing, weeping and throwing himself down before the house of God, a large crowd of Israelites—men, women and children—gathered around him. They too wept bitterly."

Also pray James 5:16, "Therefore confess your sins to each other and pray for each other so that you may be healed. The prayer of a righteous person is powerful and effective"

And 1 Peter 1:22, "Now that you have purified yourselves by obeying the truth so that you have sincere love for each other, love one another deeply, from the heart."

"When a leader falls, this opens the door for others to confess their hidden sins," said the spouse of one church leader. "We have the opportunity to model forgiveness, grace, and mercy . . . the entire congregation rallies together and forges a deeper bond. Despite the pain and mess, God will work for good in these situations."[278]

Tool Box

In 2012, NASCAR driver Danica Patrick was named the most popular driver in the Nationwide Series. The following day on Facebook, she announced her plans to divorce her husband of seven years. Rumors spread for several months before she confirmed her "relationship" [affair] with NASCAR rookie Ricky Stenhouse Jr.[279]

Prayer: Pray for your pastor to stick with his or her spouse until death separates them.

Scriptures: "May you rejoice in the wife of your youth" *(Proverbs 5:18).*

Casualties

Addictions and affairs affect far more than the hooked minister. The exhaustion from hiding sin often leaves the individual depressed.

It can be difficult to live with someone suffering from depression. Although all sin is serious, addictions and sins of a sexual nature seem to have far-reaching effects.

As the apostle Paul said, "Flee from sexual immorality. All other sins a person commits are outside the body, but whoever sins sexually, sins against their own body. Do you not know that your bodies are temples of the Holy Spirit, who is in you, whom you have received from God? You are not your own" (1 Corinthians 6:18–19).

Sexual sins run deep into the soul. They scorch the innermost part of a believers being. The spirit is left dry and empty.

Family members experience deep pain and are often pulled into the financial problems and humiliation over the ordeal. They may feel scrutinized by others because of their loved one's wrongdoing. Spouses may feel betrayed. Some may try to take the blame for the offender's actions.

Shelly Duffer serves as a board member of her church and of 127 Worldwide, which ministers to the needs of orphans and widows. After her student minister husband's arrest for sex crimes, she wanted her church to know she was all right and decided to attend worship services one more time. She arrived a little late and entered a side door to avoid interactions. Duffer planned to leave right after the sermon and never see the congregation again.

She writes: "But that was not God's plan. At the end of the sermon, an older couple approached me. Then a student. Then another came. Some spoke, others slipped money into my trembling hands. I shook, not just with tears, but with the sheer magnitude of grace. The line stretched down the aisle and around the sanctuary. They expressed grief and concern for me and my children. Some said nothing at all, but just held me. Thus began the slow, tedious journey toward healing."

The church provided experts to help the Duffers both legally and biblically face their circumstances. They allowed Duffer and her four children to live in the parsonage and passed along job leads. The church gave the kids food, clothing, and Christmas presents.[280]

Prayers for Healing for the Pastor's Family

Self-Awareness. Pray family members will realize their need for healing and get help.

Pray Psalm 119:28, "My soul is weary with sorrow; strengthen me according to your word"

And Jeremiah 31:25–26, "'I will refresh the weary and satisfy the faint.' At this I awoke and looked around. My sleep had been pleasant to me."

One pastor's wife said, "Don't stop with just seeking help for your husband. You are wounded and bleeding. Your heart has been broken and you need to know this 'thing' is not your fault. Get counseling and encouragement for yourself. It will be the best investment you ever make. Also, ask God to bring an encourager into your life who understands and can love you back to health."[281]

Forgiveness. Pray family members will forgive and not harbor anger or bitterness toward those who hurt them.

Pray Genesis 50:17, 20, "I ask you to forgive your brothers the sins and the wrongs they committed in treating you so badly" and "You intended to harm me, but God intended it for good."

Also pray Acts 8:23, "For I see that you are full of bitterness and captive to sin."

A minister's wife named Karen wrote, "Be honest with God. Tell him exactly how you feel, no matter how ugly, mean or hateful it is. He knows anyway, and he's big enough to handle it."[282]

Encouragement from Others. Ask God to move in the hearts of leaders and those in the pew (of the current church or a new church) to encourage and meet the needs of the family.

Pray 1 Thessalonians 5:14, "And we urge you, brothers and sisters, warn those who are idle and disruptive, encourage the disheartened, help the weak, be patient with everyone."

Also pray Psalm 147:3, "He heals the brokenhearted and binds up their wounds."

Shelly Duffer said, "They didn't push, but allowed us to heal at God's speed. For a long time, that meant just allowing us to attend church quietly, our hurting souls being fed by preaching and corporate worship."[283]

Culprits

Some clergy are forced out of the church even though they did nothing to deserve dismissal. A downturn in a community's economy may cause families to move in droves or reduce a family's income from two to one. Such economic disruption may force a church to lay off staff members.

Some pastors facing health issues such as dementia may be unable to continue in ministry. A gentle church board may need to release the pastor, then offer assistance until retirement. These are difficult situations.

But conditions that lead to a pastor being fired for no doctrinal or moral cause result in heartbreak for the pastoral family, staff, and members. If done in a mean-spirited manner, hearts may be shattered. No counselor but God can repair them.

The following are a few of these tragic stories.

—•—

Joel Hunter was released from his first ministry job because the congregation didn't have money for both his salary and new carpeting. Hunter is now a senior pastor for Northland, A Church Distributed, which has three campuses in central Florida.[284]

—•—

At a church in North Carolina, John (not his real name) went to church for a prayer service and routine business meeting. When the business meeting was called to order, a member of the congregation asked John and his wife to leave the sanctuary while a "sensitive matter was discussed."

Two hours later he was terminated. No charges had been brought against John's character or doctrine. The action violated the church's constitution and bylaws. John was not allowed on church property unless accompanied by one of the trustees. He was given one month's salary at his parting.[285]

—•—

Pastor Mark remembers a time two years ago when an elder began to criticize him while his daughter was deathly ill. The elder enlisted the music minister and several members from the congregation to criticize the pastor's salary, his family lifestyle, and the effectiveness of his leadership of the church.

The battle that ensued wearied Mark to the point where he wondered if he should "leave the church, leave the ministry, or leave planet Earth altogether."[286]

—•—

For five years Minister Mike (not his real name) served as a pastor in Virginia. He endured the trauma of a volatile quarterly business meeting, which focused on his effectiveness as pastor. He and his wife were asked to wait in his study during the meeting. They were not given an opportunity to respond to any derogatory comments made against his ministry. Although Mike was not fired that night, he was told to immediately look for another position.[287]

———•———

A small faction of disgruntled members at Andy's church bypassed the church's leaders and complained to the denominational authority. They criticized Andy because he had not visited enough parishioners and because the visits he did make were "unsatisfactory."

Further, they said he had "made too many changes without going through the [board]." The denomination referred the faction back to the church committee that oversees pastors.

After many unproductive meetings, the disgruntled faction that demanded Andy's continued employment be decided by a congregational vote. The Sunday of the vote, many people whom Andy did not recognize were in attendance.

Andy later found out they were inactive members who had been recruited by the faction. Many of the pastor's supporters were new believers or new to the church and had not yet become members. Therefore, they could not vote. Andy became the fifth pastor in a row forced out of the church.[288]

———•———

These moving stories can evoke a great deal of emotion. You might have personally experienced the turmoil of a church who fired its minister. Even now you may feel anger, shock, disbelief, or even a desire to take action against the guilty party in these stories.

So before we continue to pray, will you join me to check our hearts? Let's see if our thoughts about church ousters are pure.

Remember Hebrews 4:12, "For the word of God is alive and active. Sharper than any double-edged sword, it penetrates even to dividing soul and spirit, joints and marrow; it judges the thoughts and attitudes of the heart." We will pray with a clean heart after we learn more about this disheartening issue.

In July 2015, the National Association of Evangelicals reported that 18 percent of high-level ministry leaders and 5 percent of volunteers have been forced out of their ministry positions.[289]

As we have seen, some clergy do indeed need to be ousted for sexual misconduct, financial malfeasance, heresy, and the like. However, in the cases we've just read, no wrongdoing was stated that deserved termination. In some cases, no concrete reason for the termination was given.

Instead, the pastor became "the culprit" when matters inside the church were not going well. This situation also happens in racing. Fans may become unhappy with the driver and demand a change when the team is losing.

The dynamics of a forced exit seem consistent. The undercurrent against the pastor begins with a small but vocal group of individuals who have appointed themselves as the pastoral police. This disgruntled faction operates by enlisting powerful people such as board members or staff members to their side.

If the minister or spouse tries to defend themselves, they will be accused of trying to cause a church split. The dissension builds quietly until the pastor is blindsided by complaints about his or her performance.

Generally, the group tries to speed the process to termination, ignoring the church's bylaws.[290] In churches where a pastor was kicked out, usually two or more of these factors were present.

1. The church was conflicted when the pastor arrived.
2. The congregation contained factions and a lack of unity.
3. Members and leaders had conflicting visions for the church.
4. The people resisted change, resulting in power struggles within the church.
5. Members and leaders did not know how to deal with conflict.

If these issues are not resolved, the church may become a repeat offender, relieving minister after minister of duty.[291]

A few years ago, a cartoon in *Leadership Journal* depicted a pastoral search committee seated around a conference table. A committee member said, "Basically, we're looking for an innovative pastor with a fresh vision who will inspire our church to remain exactly the same."[292] This drawing aptly summarized the conflicted motives present within some congregations.

The reasons pastors are wrongly criticized include: (1) vengeance for an unconfirmed offense, (2) turning a small matter into an offense, (3) loyalty to a beloved former pastor, (4) jealousy by a wannabe preacher in the pew, (5) projecting guilt on the pastor for something the church member has failed to do, or (6) unconfessed sin. Factions within a church may form around the individual tastes or preferences of members rather than biblical truth.

The biggest hurt usually stems from the fact the pastor is accused by brothers and sisters in Christ.

No one described the pain of being attacked by one's own people better than King David in Psalm 55:12–14, "If an enemy were insulting me, I could endure it; if a foe were rising against me, I could hide. But it is you, a man like myself, my companion, my close friend, with whom I once enjoyed sweet fellowship at the house of God, as we walked about among worshipers."

Sometimes the worst part of the ordeal for clergy and their families is the period between the forced resignation or firing and the actual departure. Leaving a church can involve vacating a parsonage with no place to go and no salary. The search for a new pastorate may take six months to a year.

And some former parishioners can be downright cruel. This sometimes happens when the congregation is not informed of the true reasons for the termination. In the absence of facts, they operate on rumors.

Rodney Crowell, after his forced exit and before he moved his family, heard this message on his answering machine "Why aren't you gone by now?" Later, Crowell discovered the upholstery in his car had been slashed.[293]

Insults and cruel treatment aren't always reserved for the pastor alone. The spouse and children may be verbally assaulted as well.

Almost as devastating as being forced to exit a congregation is serving in one that does not provide pastoral care for the pastor. Paul David Tripp, in his book *Dangerous Calling*, tells of meeting with a church board after a weekend conference. The previous week, the pastor showed up very late to a weekly leadership meeting. When he did arrive, he stated the following, then left:

> "I'm done, I can't do this anymore. I can't deal with the pressures of ministry. I can't face preaching another sermon. I can't deal with another meeting. If I am honest, I would have to say that all I want to do is leave. I want to leave the ministry, I want to leave this area, and I want to leave my wife. No, there's

been no affair. I'm just tired of pretending that I'm someone I'm not. I'm tired of acting like I'm okay when I'm not. I'm tired of playing as if my marriage is good when it is the polar opposite of good. I can't preach this coming Sunday, and have to get away alone or I'm going to explode. I'm sorry to lay this on you this way, but I'm done—I can't go on."

Stunned by what they heard, the leadership team talked and prayed together. They called their pastor back and began to learn what had gone awry. Tripp spoke with them about getting to know their pastor and what pressures had drained him. Tripp gave instructions about basic pastoral care by the members for their minister.[294] A pastor who has not received TLC from the congregation may wind up feeling as hurt as if he had been forced out. No minister wants to be a quitter and leave the ministry.

It does not matter whether our pastors have been injured by conflict, criticism, or lack of care; the hemorrhaging must be stopped. Our clergy need our encouragement, care, and, most of all, our prayers.

Prayers for Those Forced Out or Lacking Care

In addition to the prayer points listed here, also pray the Prayers of Healing and Restoration and Prayers for the Restoring of the Pastor's Family noted above.

Unity. Pray for unity among the pastor and other leaders, as well as with the church family.

Pray 2 Chronicles 30:12, "Also in Judah the hand of God was on the people to give them unity of mind to carry out what the king and his officials had ordered, following the word of the LORD"

And John 17:23, "I in them and you in me—so that they may be brought to complete unity. Then the world will know that you sent me and have loved them even as you have loved me."

Paul David Tripp reports, "Most of the people you serve will love and appreciate you and will encourage you as they are able, but not all of them. Some will love you and have a wonderful plan for your life! Some will assign themselves to be the critics of your preaching and/or leadership. Some will be loyal and supportive, and some will do things that undermine your pastoral leadership . . . some will give way to the temptation to talk behind your back."[295]

Wisdom for Conflict Resolution. Ask the Father to teach your minister how to biblically deal with conflict.

Pray Proverbs 10:12, "Hatred stirs up conflict, but love covers over all wrongs"

And Proverbs 15:1, "A gentle answer turns away wrath, but a harsh word stirs up anger."

Also pray Proverbs 15:18, "A hot-tempered person stirs up conflict, but the one who is patient calms a quarrel."

Pray Proverbs 16:28, "A perverse person stirs up conflict, and a gossip separates close friends"

And Matthew 18:15, "If your brother or sister sins, go and point out their fault, just between the two of you. If they listen to you, you have won them over."

Al and Phyllis Grounds of Restored Ministries wrote, "Unsettled conflict results in people warring against each other and eventually choosing sides. The moment you sense something is wrong, you need to call in the parties involved and sit them down to work it out. When you wait, problems persist and grow. When it's left alone, it becomes like blood poisoning, eventually filtering through the entire church."[296]

Discernment in Moving On. Pray pastors will have wisdom and discernment when they interview for new ministry opportunities. Pray he or she will have courage to ask the hard questions about why the last pastor left, how many pastors the church has had in the last ten years, and the relationships of member to members, members to leaders, and leaders to leaders.

Pray your pastor will seek God earnestly about where to serve.

Pray Proverbs 2:6, "For the LORD gives wisdom; from his mouth come knowledge and understanding"

And Daniel 2:21, "He gives wisdom to the wise and knowledge to the discerning."

Leith Anderson, president of the National Association of Evangelicals, said, "Churches often don't have adequate skill or experience to handle difficult pastoral issues, and few are wise with terminations. There are tendencies to follow the advice of a dominant internal leader, fantasize that the departing pastors will be replaced by someone much better, elevate money over persons, and fail to see the long-term consequences of poorly handled terminations. The best advice to avoid pastoral terminations is to devote significant prayer, time, budget and process into calling the right pastors in the first place."[297]

Discernment in Caring. Ask God to reveal to members how to care for their minister.

Pray Philippians 2:25, "But I think it is necessary to send back to you Epaphroditus, my brother, coworker and fellow soldier, who is also your messenger, whom you sent to take care of my needs"

And Mark 15:40–41, "Some women were watching from a distance. Among them were Mary Magdalene, Mary the mother of James the younger and of Joseph, and Salome. In Galilee these women had followed him [Jesus] and cared for his needs."

"Pastors need your care—no matter how old, seasoned, gifted, or confident," said Jason Helopoulos, associate pastor at University Reformed Church.[298]

Patience in Prayer

These heartbreaking issues of prayer for our broken pastors can become overwhelming for the individual prayer warrior. We must not lose heart! In order to cope with the demands of intercession for the needs of our clergy, we, the warriors, also need help.

The next chapter explains how to start a prayer team, group, or huddle, and how to recruit intercessors for the group. We need the encouragement of others to keep us faithful in praying for our pastors.

11

Passing It On

Recruiting Pit Crew Members

―――――――◆―――――――

WINNING WISDOM
Heaven is full of answers to prayer for which
no one ever bothered to ask.
BILLY GRAHAM

―――――――◆―――――――

Mike McClure, a former WWE prospect, traveled to Michigan International Speedway to watch a race. He was recruited for the Hendrick Motorsports developmental pit crew program. Having suffered debilitating injuries in his quest to become a pro wrestler, McClure chose to pursue the opportunity with Hendrick. A former All-American wrestler at Michigan State University, and an All-American in academics, McClure now hones his craft as a fueler and jackman.[299]

Joe Gibbs Racing (JGR) runs a similar recruiting program. JGR looks for college athletes who are not only strong but also have a winning mentality. Pit crew recruits come from many different collegiate sports, including wrestling, football, track and field, basketball, and softball. Intense training in this program incorporates weight lifting, running, exercising, and drills to prepare crew members for a fifteen-second pit stop.[300]

My prayer for you as you read this book is that your prayer muscles will develop. Muscles need to be stretched and exercised regularly. Prayer also needs to be practiced constantly, as the apostle Paul reminds us in 1 Thessalonians 5:17: "Pray continually."

Second, I pray your faith will increase to the point Matthew 21:22 becomes a reality in your life: "If you believe, you will receive whatever you ask for in prayer."

The NASCAR world calls believing and working toward a desired outcome a "winning mentality." The Bible dubs this attitude as expectancy.

Psalm 5:3 says, "In the morning, LORD, you hear my voice; in the morning I lay my requests before you and wait expectantly." A prayer warrior's enthusiasm and passion for prayer keeps growing as he or she sees prayers answered.

We have learned many of the issues our pastors face in their day-to-day service. We have interceded for our ministers using the prayer lists provided. We want to keep praying until our pastors go the distance and finish the race.

"I have fought the good fight, I have finished the race, I have kept the faith" (2 Timothy 4:7).

In their book *The Battle Plan for Prayer*, Stephen and Alex Kendrick wrote:

"All pastors need an army of prayer warriors in their churches lifting them up. Their work is eternal and vital. Their calling is draining and demanding. The expectations on them are endless. They are commanded by God to be diligent and sacrificial. Devoted and faithful. Passionate and pure. Genuinely seeking to honor the Lord and reach their communities through the serving and equipping of their congregations. Yet the enemy more intensely attacks them. He paints a bright red target on them and their families and tries to wear them down to derail their homes, health, and ministries. Much of their service is visible, but many of their responsibilities are private—laboring in study, providing spiritual counsel, peacemaking a never-ending stream of conflict. They carry a heavy load amid murmuring opposition. So they can grow discouraged and overwhelmed under the weight of a good work. Like Aaron and Hur did for Moses, we should faithfully lift up their arms in prayer, knowing their own strength is not enough" (Exodus 17:11–12).[301]

We are excited to pray for our clergy, but overwhelmed. We know prayer is worth the time and effort. We cannot do this alone. We must recruit help.

Work through Existing Groups

In some churches, prayers groups are already in place. Encourage and enlist these existing groups to pray for pastors by passing on prayer items and verses from this book. If you are a leader or member of a small group, suggest group members use *Pit Crew* as a basis for study, discussion, and prayer.

October is designated Pastor Appreciation Month. Ask permission from your leadership board or Pastor Appreciation Committee to make a thirty-day prayer list available to members of your congregation. Most of all, pray about how God wants you to motivate other prayer warriors to pray for your minister.

Dan Reiland previously served as executive pastor at Skyline Church in San Diego, where he recruited thirty prayer partners, one for each day of the month. For the last fourteen years, he served at 12Stone Church in Lawrenceville, Georgia. At 12Stone, seven prayer partners pray for Reiland one for each day of the week. Reiland counts on these warriors to move heaven on his behalf.[302]

Ask seven people to sign up to pray one day a week for your minister for six months or a year. Then provide them with prayer lists or a copy of this book. Remember to text or email them, reminding them of your thanks and encouraging their faithfulness in prayer. Repeat the process. Most likely, the majority of the seven will sign up again.

Pit to Pulpit

In 1992, Barna found the median age of pastors was forty-four. In a 2017 research study, Barna reported the median age of pastors to be fifty-four.[303]

Prayer: Pray for God to call our teens and young adults into ministry.

Scripture: "Then he said to his disciples, 'The harvest is plentiful but the workers are few. Ask the Lord of the harvest, therefore, to send out workers into his harvest field'" *(Matthew 9:37–38).*

Start a Prayer Group

If your assembly does not have an organized prayer ministry, consider starting a prayer meeting. The first step is to pray for God to bring members. Remember, two is a group. Begin by asking the pastor's spouse. An advertisement in the church bulletin or newsletter, posting a sign, or using social media can be effective methods to gain warriors.

Determine when and where you will meet and be specific as to place and time: in your home every Thursday evening at seven o'clock or in classroom 201 every other Saturday morning at nine o'clock. Your group could meet during the hour before services every Sunday or during the second worship service.

Be creative. The possibilities are numerous. Pick up the phone and have a prayer conference every Thursday evening. Ladies in my neighborhood walk the streets in our subdivision as they pray.

As Dietrich Bonhoeffer wrote, "It is in fact the most normal thing in the common Christian life to pray together."[304]

When you advertise or ask, present your vision of the prayer time. As Phillip challenged Nathanael to see Jesus of Nazareth the first time, tell them to "come and see" (John 1:46).

Receive every "No" graciously. Trust God to change schedules or clear up issues so those folks may eventually join the team. Select a place free of distractions. Most prayer meetings meet for an hour or two, especially if the partners are mature prayer warriors. Do not cancel the prayer gathering even if only one or two will be present. Your commitment will demonstrate the importance of praying for your pastor.

When intercessors or their children are sick, or out of town, remember life happens. Rather than scolding those who are absent, encourage and thank those who do attend. Keep requests in the strictest confidence. Shred old request lists. Gossip of any kind cannot be tolerated. If someone does share hearsay, talk with them in private.

After I had spoken twice to a member about her gossip, I ended a prayer huddle early when another rumor slipped out. The group had become so toxic I terminated the meetings altogether. A few months later, I started another prayer group.

Lead a Prayer Group

As a leader, pray regularly for your group to develop unity and grow in love for each other. Keep a contact list so you can notify members of significant answers to their intercessions between meetings, or of any changes in your meeting place. Keep a journal of prayer requests and their answers.

As your huddle increases, consider enlisting a co-leader for help and support. If your prayer group mushrooms, divide the group and let the co-leader become a new huddle leader. Allow the co-leader and other mature warriors to occasionally lead the meeting.

Do not let the group become dependent on you. If you become ill, you do not want the prayer huddle to drift apart while you recuperate. As much as possible, stick to the schedule and wrap up on time. Keep the group safe by letting members know they do not have to pray out loud.

The best way to keep people coming back is to vary the methods of prayer. Bring some prayer points with related verses. Open with a song of praise, a verse, a short passage of scripture, or a brief period of quiet reflection. Read from your journal the prayers that were answered. Start your meeting with thanksgiving and praise for these answers.

Another opening could include reading a short passage on prayer from any of the following books:

Prayer by Richard Foster

With Christ in the School of Prayer by Andrew Murray

If You Will Ask by Oswald Chambers

The Complete Works of E. M. Bounds by E. M. Bounds

Too Busy Not to Pray by Bill Hybels

The Battle Plan for Prayer by Stephen and Alex Kendrick

During a meeting, direct the group to pray through a prayer list in *Pit Crew*. The following week, guide the group to pray through a Psalm for your minister. Prayer time can be uplifting and effective when you softly play praise music and let the members pray silently.

Another idea is to give each intercessor a three-by-five-inch card and instruct them to write the letters P, A, S, T, O, R down the left side. Then ask them to write a prayer request to match each letter. Other acrostics for prayer could be *shepherd*, *preacher*, or *minister*. Bring each request or verse on a piece of paper, then pass the hat and let each warrior pick a prayer item to pray out loud or silently. For those who pray silently, instruct them to say "Silently" before they pray and "Next" when they finish. If someone does not have anything to pray or add, they can also say, "Next."

Take a field trip and pray while gathered around the pastor's pulpit, study, or office. Do a prayer walk around your minister's home. (Ask permission and make sure all members of the household are aware of what's happening.)

If you have a talker in your group, try having each member write down personal requests on a three-by-five-inch card. Pass the cards to the leader, who will email these requests to the members later in the week. If there is an urgent request, gather around the member and pray on the spot.

Encourage those with a funny or interesting story to save it for the end of the meeting. If some members intercede with lengthy prayers, guide your warriors in a meeting with sentence prayers. If going around the circle in prayer seems boring, try popcorn prayer—having members pop up with brief prayers.

Be imaginative in finding ways to involve your intercessors. Ask volunteers to bring a Bible verse about prayer to read and open the meeting. Ask volunteers to bring three-by-five-inch cards. Invite members to share something they learned about prayer in their personal devotions. Have a quiet member hand out the prayer list.

Know the Power of Prayer

Tool Box

NASCAR rules allow stock cars to be no more than 725 horsepower. This pales in comparison to the power of prayer, which we cannot measure.[305]

Prayer: Pray that the members of your huddle begin to grasp the power of their prayers.

Scriptures: "The prayer of a righteous person is powerful and effective" *(James 5:16)*.

Remember the power of prayer remains more important than the methods.

In Ephesians 6:19–20, Paul pleads, "Pray also for me, that whenever I speak, words may be given me so that I will fearlessly make known the mystery of the gospel for which I am an ambassador in chains. Pray that I may declare it fearlessly, as I should."

Paul knew his ministry would only continue if people of the church prayed for him. Prayer maintained his health in prison. Prayer brought servants to transcribe the epistles he wrote. Prayer preserved those writings for our Bibles today. Prayer allowed him to fearlessly witness to guards. Prayer lifted his spirits.

Stephen and Alex Kendrick wrote:

> "Prayer is privileged access to the God of the universe, bought and paid for by the blood of His Son on our account for all those who freely receive Him as Lord.
>
> Prayer is what frames our pressing, short-term issues with God's eternal perspective, showing us just how temporary—and endurable, and winnable— even our most intense battles truly are. Prayer means hope. Prayer means help. Prayer means relief. Prayer means power.
>
> And a lot of it."[306]

Commit to Pray

When you were young, remember the last minute directions your mom gave as you left the house? These were words of wisdom she did not want you to forget. Years later you have realized their importance. In fact, you probably shared them with your own children.

The apostle Paul penned final instructions in the closing of 1 Thessalonians. Three of these directives are admonitions to care and pray for your minister:

> "Now we ask you, brothers and sisters, to acknowledge those who work hard among you, who

care for you in the Lord and who admonish you"
(5:12).

"Hold them in the highest regard in love because
of their work. Live in peace with each other" (5:13).

"Brothers and sisters, pray for us" (5:25).

We need to heed Paul's guidelines which also are words of
wisdom.

My prayer for you, beloved intercessor, is that you will commit
to the Lord to become a faithful member of the pit crew. Tell several
trustworthy friends of your commitment to pray regularly for your
shepherd so they can hold you accountable.

Place a reminder in your home or office. This might be a prayer
list with your devotional materials, a verse to pray on a three-by-
five-inch card attached to your refrigerator, or a small stock car in
a spot you will see every day. Your commitment will move your
pastor across the finish line of his or her journey. Your pledge to pray
regularly will also bring your prayer life up to speed.

Surprisingly, I learned about the tremendous horsepower of
prayer and the importance of making a commitment to pray for our
ministers at my father's funeral. About the time my father went into
the hospital with terminal cancer, his pastor took a new position and
moved to a nearby community to minister to retirees.

When my dad's friend and former minister officiated his services,
Brother John told family and friends of his last visit to my dad's
bedside. After chatting for a while, the pastor asked, "Can I pray?"

In a severely weakened state from his malignancies, my father
stood, trembling. With tubing, cords, and cables stretched across the
bed, and short of breath, my father prayed for his brother in Christ
and his new ministry.

APPENDIX

Prayer for Pastoral Responsibility

1. **Thank God for our pastors.**

    "So Christ himself gave the apostles, the prophets, the evangelists, the pastors and teachers, to equip his people for works of service, so that the body of Christ may be built up until we all reach unity in the faith and in the knowledge of the Son of God and become mature, attaining to the whole measure of the fullness of Christ" (Ephesians 4:11–13).

2. **Thank God they serve us.**

    "This, then, is how you ought to regard us: as servants of Christ and as those entrusted with the mysteries God has revealed" (1 Corinthians 4:1).

    "For what we preach is not ourselves, but Jesus Christ as Lord, and ourselves as your servants for Jesus' sake" (2 Corinthians 4:5).

3. **Pray we will honor them as they work hard and challenge us.**

"Now we ask you, brothers and sisters, to acknowledge those who work hard among you, who care for you in the Lord and who admonish you" (1 Thessalonians 5:12).

4. **Thank the Lord they watch out for us. Pray we will support them in prayer to help lighten their loads.**

"Have confidence in your leaders and submit to their authority, because they keep watch over you as those who must give an account. Do this so that their work will be a joy, not a burden, for that would be of no benefit to you. Pray for us" (Hebrews 13:17–18).

5. **Thank God for their faithful preaching, teaching and encouragement as we mature in Christ. Pray we will be attentive to the message God sends through our pastors.**

"For the lips of a priest ought to preserve knowledge, because he is the messenger of the LORD Almighty and people seek instruction from his mouth" (Malachi 2:7).

"I have become its servant by the commission God gave me to present to you the word of God in its fullness. . . . the mystery that has been kept hidden for ages and generations, but is now disclosed to the Lord's people. . . . He is the one we proclaim, admonishing and teaching everyone with all wisdom, so that we may present everyone fully mature in Christ" (Colossians 1:25, 26, 28).

6. **Pray God will help us value our pastors and remember to pray for them as they are human and fallible. Pray they will be infused with the power of God.**

"But we have this treasure in jars of clay to show that this all-surpassing power is from God and not from us" (2 Corinthians 4:7).

7. **Pray the enemy is not able to destroy, detour, detain, or discourage our pastors. Thank God for their example to our congregations in standing firm.**

"Be alert and of sober mind. Your enemy the devil prowls around like a roaring lion looking for someone to devour. Resist him, standing firm in the faith, because you know that the family of believers throughout the world is undergoing the same kind of sufferings" (1 Peter 5:8–9).

Prayer List Courtesy of *Pit Crew: Praying for Our Pastors to Finish the Race,* ©2017 Sally U. Smith.

Permeated with Scripture

Pray these Scriptures for our pastors:

"Blessed are they whose ways are blameless, who walk according to the law of the LORD. Blessed are they who keep his statutes and seek him with all their heart" (Psalm 119:1–2).

"I will proclaim the name of the LORD. Oh, praise the greatness of our God! He is the Rock, his works are perfect, and all his ways are just. A faithful God who does no wrong, upright and just is he" (Deuteronomy 32:3–4).

"I have not stopped giving thanks for you, remembering you in my prayers. I keep asking that the God of our Lord Jesus Christ, the glorious Father, may give you the Spirit of wisdom and revelation, so that you may know him better. I pray that the eyes of your heart may be enlightened in order that you may know the hope to which he has called you, the riches of his glorious inheritance in his holy people, and his incomparably great power for us who believe." (Ephesians 1:16–19).

"And this is my prayer: that your love may abound more and more in knowledge and depth of insight, so that you may be able to discern what is best and may be pure and blameless until the day of Christ, filled with the fruit of righteousness that comes through Jesus Christ—to the glory and praise of God" (Philippians 1:9–11).

"For this reason, since the day we heard about you, we have not stopped praying for you. We continually ask God to fill you with the knowledge of his will through all the wisdom and understanding that the Spirit gives, so that you may live a life worthy of the Lord and please him in every way: bearing fruit in every good work, growing in the knowledge of God, being strengthened with all power according to his glorious might so that you may have great endurance and patience, and giving joyful thanks to the Father, who has qualified you to share in the inheritance of his holy people in the kingdom of light" (Colossians 1:9–12).

"Call to me and I will answer you and tell you great and unsearchable things you do not know" (Jeremiah 33:3).

"However, as it is written: 'What no eye has seen, what no ear has heard, and what no human mind has conceived'—the things God has prepared for those who love him—these are the things God has revealed to us by his Spirit. The Spirit searches all things, even the deep things of God" (1 Corinthians 2:9–10).

Pick a special verse of yours. Write it here:

Use this favorite verse to pray for your pastor.

Prayer List Courtesy of *Pit Crew: Praying for Our Pastors to Finish the Race,* ©2017 Sally U. Smith.

Personal Walk with God

Prayers from the Book of Colossians

1. Lord, help our pastors to give thanks in all things and to make prayer a priority (1:3).
2. Develop in our pastors a strong faith in you and a love for all the saints (1:4).
3. Like the Colossians, I pray [pastors' names] will keep bearing fruit and growing (1:6).
4. Fill our pastors with the knowledge of your will through spiritual wisdom and understanding (1:9).
5. Show Pastors [names] how to conduct themselves in ways that honor and please you. Help them to increase in their knowledge of you (1:10).
6. Help our pastors to be strengthened with your power so they may be steadfast and patient (1:11).
7. I pray our pastors' sufferings will spill over into joyfully thanking you they are allowed to share in your blessings (1:12).
8. Remind our pastors they are delivered from darkness and brought into the kingdom of your beloved Son (1:13).
9. We pray you will be foremost in everything in our pastors' lives (1:18).
10. Father, we ask you to make their faith sturdy, rock solid, and fixed on the hope of the gospel (1:23).
11. Please knit [pastors' names] hearts together in love with other brothers and sisters in Christ (2:2).
12. In our pastors' lives, build discipline and steadfast faith in you (2:5).

13. Cause them to be deeply rooted in you and possess a heart overflowing with gratitude (2:7).

14. Lord, dwell in [pastors' names] so they will be made complete (2:10).

15. We pray our pastors will set their affections on heavenly things rather than worldly (3:2).

16. Turn [pastors' names] away from immorality, impurity, lust, evil desires, greed and idolatry (3:5).

17. Lead them to get rid of anger, wrath, malice, slander and abusive speech (3:8).

18. Help them to not lie, but to live lives of integrity (3:9).

19. May their lives demonstrate compassion, kindness, humility, gentleness and patience (3:12).

20. Humbly remembering how you have forgiven them, teach our pastors how to forgive and be at peace with others, (3:13).

21. Lord, make their lives to be known by love, which will bond them in unity (3:14).

22. We pray our pastors' hearts will be controlled by the peace of Christ (3:15).

23. May your Word permeate their lives as they encourage others and worship you (3:16).

24. We pray all of their words and actions will reflect your name for his glory (3:17).

25. Help [pastors' names] to grow in love and understanding of their spouses and children (3:19, 21).

26. We pray our pastors' children will please the Lord by obeying their parents (3:20).

27. As they work, let our pastors serve robustly for you rather than to impress people (3:23).

28. Help our pastors devote themselves to prayer, keeping alert, and having an attitude of thanksgiving (4:2).

29. Teach them to be wise and a good example to outsiders. I pray they will make the most of every opportunity to share Christ with others (4:5).
30. Let our pastors' speech be gracious, and may they respond with encouragement (4:6).
31. We pray our pastors will persevere in doing the ministry you have called them to do. Lord, enable them to complete it (4:17).

Prayer List Courtesy of *Pit Crew: Praying for Our Pastors to Finish the Race,* ©2017 Sally U. Smith.

Pastoral Roles

Sunday—Preacher/Teacher.

Pray our pastors will be anointed of the Spirit in their preaching. Pray their preaching will be saturated with the very words of God, will exalt and glorify Christ, and will bring the lost to Christ and transform lives. (Psalm 34:3; Romans 10:15; 12:1–2; Ephesians 6:19; 1 Peter 4:11)

Monday—Personal Walk

Pray our pastors will seek after God's heart through Bible study, meditation, and prayer. Pray their spirit-led walk with God will be characterized by worship, righteousness, holiness, humility, and obedience. (Psalm 1:2; 84:11; Proverbs 15:33; Jeremiah 7:23; Romans 2:4; Galatians 5:25; 1 Thessalonians 5:18; Hebrews 12:28)

Tuesday—Pastoral Care

Pray our pastors will exemplify the compassion of the Good Shepherd. Pray they will comfort, counsel, and protect, through the power of the Comforter, the hurting, weak, feeble, and needy souls in our congregations. (Isaiah 40:11; Jeremiah 3:15; John 10:11–15; 14:26–27)

Wednesday—Prophet

Pray the Word of God will be revealed to our pastors. Pray God's vision for their local assemblies will be made known to them and they will make it clear to the congregation. (1 Corinthians 14:26–39; Ephesians 3:6; 6:19–20; Colossians 2:2–3; 2 Timothy 4:1–2;)

Thursday—Pastoral Leadership

Pray our pastors will be servant-leaders who direct and lead the staff and volunteers with Spirit-led sensitivity. Pray they will exercise wisdom, diligence, mercy, and compassion in all their dealings with people as they have oversight of projects and programs. (1 Kings 3:9, 28; Zechariah 7:9–10; 2 Corinthians 8:16–21; Romans 12:8)

Friday —Priest and Evangelist

Pray our pastors will be diligent in their intercession for their congregations. Pray our pastors will be examples and teachers who demonstrate how to lead souls to Christ. (Psalm 9:9–11; Ephesians 6:18–20; Romans10:11, 15; Acts 1:8)

Saturday—Pastor's Family

Pray our pastors' families will be a priority. Pray they will cherish time at home as they are mutually blessed and protected. Pray their spouses and kids will be supportive of their ministries. (Psalm 91:15–16; Ephesians 4:32; 5:25, 33)

Prayers of Protection

From the armor of God found in Ephesians 6:10–18:

"Finally, be strong in the Lord and in his mighty power. Put on the full armor of God, so that you can take your stand against the devil's schemes. For our struggle is not against flesh and blood, but against the rulers, against the authorities, against the powers of this dark world and against the spiritual forces of evil in the heavenly realms. Therefore put on the full armor of God, so that when the day of evil comes, you may be able to stand your ground, and after you have done everything, to stand. . . ."

1. **Stand firm then, with the belt of truth buckled around your waist.**

   I pray our pastors will remain an example to their congregation in standing firm. May they know the truth so they will be free from Satan's bondage. (John 8:32; Colossians 2:8)

2. **With the breastplate of righteousness in place.**

   May our shepherds not feel defeated or unworthy of their position in Christ. Lord, I pray they will accept God's gift of righteousness when they enter into spiritual warfare. (Romans 5:17; 2 Corinthians 5:21)

3. **And with your feet fitted with the readiness that comes from the gospel of peace.**

   Let the peace of God overflow from our pastors' lives so others may see heaven. I pray our shepherds will stay ready to answer their questions with the gospel. (Romans 10:13–15; 1 Peter 3:15)

4. **In addition to all this, take up the shield of faith, with which you can extinguish all the flaming arrows of the evil one.**

    Father, I pray our pastors' faith will remain strong so fear and doubt cannot enter. Help them to focus on your truth rather than circumstances or Satan's distractions. (2 Corinthians 5:7; 2 Timothy 1:7; 1 Peter 5:8–9)

5. **Take the helmet of salvation.**

    Let our pastors be filled with the Holy Spirit so their minds stay protected from wrong thoughts, desires, or feelings. Help them to recognize strongholds in their lives and in others who are at war with the knowledge of God. (2 Corinthians 10:3–5; Galatians 5:16, 25)

6. **And the sword of the Spirit, which is the word of God.**

    Lord, may our pastors' lives overflow with your Word and may their prayers become saturated with the authority of your Holy Scriptures. I pray they will use this weapon to bind Satan from their life and others. (Matthew16:19; Romans 12:2; 2 Corinthians 10:4–5; Galatians 5:24; 1 Timothy 4:13; 2 Timothy 2:24–26)

7. **And pray in the Spirit on all occasions with all kinds of prayers and requests. With this in mind, be alert and always keep on praying for all the saints.**

    I pray our pastors will stand tall as mighty men of prayer. Father, may they stay devoted to their flock in prayer. (Matthew 26:41; Acts 1:14; 6:4; Romans 8:26; Colossians 4:2; 1 Thessalonians 5:2, 17)

Prayer List Courtesy of *Pit Crew: Praying for Our Pastors to Finish the Race,* ©2017 Sally U. Smith.

Pray for Peer Relationships

F–Fun Friend

Lord, I pray our pastors will cultivate good relationships. Help them to find friends who are loyal and stick with them. May these friends bring joy to their hearts as they share interests and laughter together. Teach our pastors how to love. (Proverbs 12:26; 18:24; 17:22; John 13:34–35; 1 Corinthians 13:4–7)

R–Reporter

Father, I pray our pastors will develop a friend who will report the truth to them about their attitudes and behaviors. May this friend tell them what they need to hear not what they want to hear, and may their companion do so in love. I pray they will receive any criticism or rebuke graciously, examine it carefully, and then maintain the courage and endurance to change. (2 Samuel 12:13; Psalm 51:1–2; 139:23–24; Proverbs 24:26; 27:5–6; 28:23; 2 Corinthians 2:4; Ephesians 4:15)

I–Intercessor

God bring people into our pastors' lives who will regularly and faithfully pray for them. I ask that these prayer warriors will intercede for protection from the enemy, for unity with coworkers, for spiritual passion, and continual renewal. Praise the Lord for warriors who volunteer to pray! (Luke 22:31–32; John 17:9, 15, 21, 24; 1 Thessalonians 5:25)

E–Encourager

Lord, I pray for an encourager like Barnabas to enter our pastors' lives. Bring them someone to accurately evaluate the things they do well and then affirm these qualities in their lives. I pray our pastors will find a comrade who will strengthen and steady them. Send them a friend to encourage their leadership and faith. (Deuteronomy 1:38; Isaiah 35:3–4; Mark 1:11; Acts 4:36; 15:32; 1 Thessalonians 3:2; Hebrews 10:24)

N–New Blood

God, bring some friends into our pastors' lives who will help share the load of ministry. I pray for energetic co-workers who will partner with them to take on part of their responsibilities and stretch them to follow your vision for the ministry. I pray these fellow soldiers will remain faithful, and will challenge our pastors to continually uphold a vibrant walk with God. (Psalm 2:14; Proverbs 27:17; 29:18; Ecclesiastes 4:9–12; Jeremiah 17:8; 2 Corinthians 8:23; Philippians 2:25; 1 Thessalonians 3:2)

D–Discipler

Father, help our pastors find a mentor who possesses trustworthiness and great wisdom. I pray this discipler will encourage them to know Christ's teachings and to apply those principles in their lives and decisions. Father, may this mentor show them how to bear fruit that glorifies you. May this discipler challenge them to completely surrender to your will in every aspect of their lives. (Luke 14:27; John 8:31–32; 15:8; Romans 7:4; James 4:7–10)

S–Shepherd

Jesus, I pray you will send a tender and compassionate shepherd who will pastor our pastors. I pray this friend will help revive and sustain our pastors' spiritual passion. I ask that our pastors will have a colleague whom they can always turn to when life gets tough. (1 Samuel 23:1; Psalm 23; Isaiah 40:11; John 10:11)

Prayer List Courtesy of *Pit Crew: Praying for Our Pastors to Finish the Race,* ©2017 Sally U. Smith.

Pray for Pastor's Family

Sunday

Lord, I pray you will be the first and foremost priority in my pastor's family. May each one have a Spirit-led walk that deepens day-by-day through Bible study and prayer. I pray they will be pure, humble, obedient, and blameless. (Psalm 1; 25:9; 119:9–11, 20; Matthew 6:33; Galatians 5:25; 1 Thessalonians 5:18, 23–24; Titus 3:1–2; 2 Peter 3:18)

Monday

Father, I pray the pastor's family will be his priority ministry. May the pastoral couple take the time to develop a strong marriage, and may the children honor their parents. I pray my shepherd's family will be willing to share the load of daily family life. Help them to serve one another and be flexible in taking care of responsibilities. (John 13:34–35; Romans 12:10, 16; Galatians 5:13–14; Ephesians 4:2, 32; 5:2, 21–33; 6:1–3; Colossians 3:13; 1 Thessalonians 5:11; Hebrews 3:13; 10:24; 1 Peter 1:22; 3:8; 1 John 3:11)

Tuesday

Lord, I pray you will help my pastor's spouse and kids to set boundaries. Give them wisdom in dealing with constantly ringing phones, filled calendars, and other issues of family privacy. Don't let peers pressure them into unrealistic expectations, but cause them to stay focused on your will for their lives (Proverbs 19:23; Ecclesiastes 3:1, 5–7; Jeremiah 29:11; Matthew 16:17; Acts 6:2–4)

Wednesday

Jesus, help every member of the family to develop good friendships that will encourage them to grow. I pray they will have friends with a listening ear and a praying heart when trouble comes. Bond them together with other ministry families. (1 Samuel 12:23; 23:16; Proverbs 17:17; 18:13–15; 27:9; Ecclesiastes 4:9–12; Hebrews 10:24–25; 13:18; James 5:16)

Thursday

Heavenly Father, I pray you will provide for every need. Help my pastor's family to not fret but to be content in all situations. Give them endurance when hard times come and they become weary. Move in the hearts of people to provide for their physical needs. Help each family member to be gracious in accepting these gifts and blessings. (Isaiah 40:29–31; Matthew 6:28–34; Luke 12:32; Philippians 4:10–20; 1 Peter 5:7)

Friday

Lord, give my pastor and his or her family insight into dealing with criticism. Help them to discern truth and to change any disobedience, wrong motives, or harmful attitudes. Lead them in applying scriptural principles of resolution. I pray they will be gracious and forgiving when others expect too much, are unkind, or are wrong in their evaluation. (Psalm 19:12–14; 91:1–2; 139:23–24; Ephesians 4:31–32; 5:1; Philippians 1:9–11; James 1:5; 1 Peter 3:13–17)

Saturday

God, I pray my pastor's spouse and kids will be supportive of his or her call to ministry. May their home be a refuge. May the spouse be their best friend and lover, chief listener, most enthusiastic cheerleader, and most diligent prayer warrior. (1 Kings 8:45, 59–60; Psalm 61:4; Philippians 3:14; James 5:16)

Prayer List Courtesy of *Pit Crew: Praying for Our Pastors to Finish the Race*, ©2017 Sally U. Smith.

Prayers for Persevering

1. Lord, I pray my pastor will be able to release the past. I pray he or she will be able to forgive all who have caused hurt. Lord begin the process to renew my minister's mind, soul and strength (Isaiah 40:31; 43:18–19; 61:4; Habakkuk 3:2; Romans 12:2; 2 Corinthians 5:17; Ephesians 4:31–32)

2. While hurting badly, help my pastor to obey you in everything. I pray he or she will keep searching your Word, praying, and following you in righteousness. (Psalm 19:14; 51:10; 119:165; Romans 12:1; 2 Corinthians 7:1; 10:5; James 1:22; 4:17; 1 John 5:21)

3. Father, I pray my shepherd will be delivered from any bondage or oppression that may be enslaving him or her. Set my pastor free. Help my minister to stand firm with the armor of God against any evil attack. (Psalm 34:19; 118:5; John 8:32, 36; Galatians 5:1; Ephesians 6:10–18; 1 Peter 5:8–9)

4. Jesus, help my pastor to keep following you step-by-step through the process of healing and restoration. Help her or him not to quit if the road to recovery goes slowly. Give my minister the courage to seek counseling. I pray she or he will be fully surrendered to what you have to teach her or him during her or his brokenness. (Psalm 16:7–8; 32:8; 51:17; 118:5; 119:116–117; Proverbs 15:22; Isaiah 28:26, 29; 57:15; Jeremiah 29:11–13; John 14:16–17)

5. Lord, I pray my pastor will understand as never before how much you love him or her. May he or she experience your grace and strength. May my shepherd find rest in you. (Psalm 33:22; 62:1; 91:1; 119:76; 136; Proverbs 3:34; Isaiah 40:29; Jeremiah 31:3; Matthew 11:28–29; Romans 8:35, 38–39; 2 Corinthians 12:9; 1 Peter 5:7)

6. When my minister is hurting, I pray you will help him or her to react properly. Keep him or her from lashing out at others in anger, a critical spirit, fear, envy, or revenge. Keep my preacher from denial, depression, anxiety, and self-pity. Help pastor to be real and not to wear masks of pride or deception. (Proverbs 15:1; 16:32; Romans 12:19; Ephesians 1:18; 4:26–27, 30; Philippians 4:6–7; James 1:22–25; 4:1–2)

7. Lord, help my pastor stand firm. I pray she or he will know God well and proclaim him as Lord of her or his life. I also pray my minister will recognize attacks from Satan and pray for God's power in her or his life. Lord may my shepherd's journey from brokenness to wholeness cause her or him to have a deeper walk with you. (Psalm 16:1–2; 119:12–16, 90; Proverbs 10:25; John 8:4;10:10; 1 Corinthians 2:9; 16:13; 2 Corinthians 11:14; Ephesians 6:12; Hebrews 13:5; James 4:6–10; 1 Peter 1:6–7; 5:10)

Prayer List Courtesy of *Pit Crew: Praying for Our Pastors to Finish the Race,* ©2017 Sally U. Smith.

Prayers for Passing It On

As you pray over these verses, write down the names of those who God brings to mind.

"Ask and it will be given to you; seek and you will find; knock and the door will be opened to you" (Matthew 7:7).

"Be devoted to one another in brotherly love. Honor one another above yourselves. Never be lacking in zeal, but keep your spiritual fervor, serving the Lord. Be joyful in hope, patient in affliction, faithful in prayer" (Romans 12:10–12).

"Whoever can be trusted with very little can also be trusted with much" (Luke 16:10).

"They all joined together constantly in prayer" (Acts 1:14).

"And whatever you do, whether in word or deed, do it all in the name of the Lord Jesus, giving thanks to God the Father through him" (Colossians 3:17).

"A gossip betrays a confidence, but a trustworthy person keeps a secret" (Proverbs 11:13).

"Finally, all of you, be like-minded, be sympathetic, love one another, be compassionate and humble" (1 Peter 3:8).

"He guides the humble in what is right and teaches them his way" (Psalm 25:9).

Possible Pit Crew Members:

Prayer List Courtesy of *Pit Crew: Praying for Our Pastors to Finish the Race,* ©2017 Sally U. Smith.

DISCUSSION QUESTIONS & ACTIVITIES

Chapter 1: Pastoral Responsibility

Read Acts 4:23–31. After Peter and John returned and reported what happened, what was the first thing the people did? What aspect of prayer was evident in verses 24–28 before they brought their requests to God?

Adoration is praise and worship to God. Begin your prayer time with praise. Use Psalm 145 or 150 to stir your thoughts and help you focus on God. Make a list of the pastors who helped in deepening your walk with your Lord. Refer to the first prayer list "Pastoral Responsibility" in the Appendix. Pray through this list and thank God for your former and present pastors.

Chapter 2: Permeated with Scripture

In the early church, new believers learned to pray by praying the Psalms. Who taught you to pray? How did they teach you? What method(s) helped you to learn how to pray?

ACTS is an acronym that stands for Adoration, Confession, Thanksgiving, and Supplication.

Use the following Psalms with the ACTS acronym for prayer time.

A–Psalm 3

C–Psalm 51:10, 12

T–Psalm 118:1, 21

S–Psalm 119:1–2

Go to the Appendix and pray through the remainder of the "Permeated with Scripture" list.

Chapter 3: Personal Walk with God

Have you personally seen an answer to prayer? Do you have a daily time of devotions scheduled (this includes Bible reading and prayer)? If not, when do you plan to start a daily quiet time with God? Is your time with God alive and fresh? If not, what steps will you take to energize your alone time with God? Would your minister be invigorated by your excitement over your devotional time?

The next prayer list in the Appendix contains thirty-one prayers based on the book of Colossians. Add these prayers to a calendar so you can pray one each day for your minster. Use the ACTS method for prayer time.

A–1 Chronicles 29:11–12

C–1 John 1:9

T–Psalm 100:4

S–"Personal Walk with God" list in the Appendix

Chapter 4: Pastoral Roles

List the roles of the senior pastor. Now put them in order of priority. Compare your list with others in the group and see if any of them match. Purchase a Matchbox or Hotwheels car (or similar) and write 2 Timothy 4:7 on the car. Place the racer in a prominent spot to remind you to intercede for your shepherd. Use the ACTS method to pray.

A–Exodus 15:1–3

C–Psalm 32:1–2

T–1 Thessalonians 5:18

S–"Pastoral Roles" list from the Appendix

Chapter 5: Protection

Name the five ways Satan tries to mislead and force your pastor out of the race. Discuss what Proverbs 22:3 means.

How did Nehemiah deal with enemies who threatened to attack (see Neh. 4:9, 16–18)?

The Five Ps of Prayer helps us to remember five actions when we pray:

Praise and honor to God, Provision for our needs, Pardon from our sins and to forgive others, Protection for all who are dear to us, and Purpose to seek his kingdom first in our lives.

Use the Five Ps of Prayer to pray for protection.

Praise–Nehemiah 9:5–6

Provision–Psalm 65:9–13

Pardon–Psalm 25:8–11

Protection–"Prayers of Protection" from the Appendix

Purpose–Matthew 6:33

Chapter 6: Peer Relationships

Read 1 Samuel 18:1–4; 19:1–7; 20:1–4; 9–13; 16–17; 32–42, then list the ways Jonathan demonstrated friendship to David. Job also had friends (see Job 2:11). When trouble came, how did Job's three friends respond (see Job 19:14, 19)?

Using the Five Ps of Prayer, petition God to give our pastors good friends to help during times of trouble.

Praise–Amos 9:5–6
Provision–"Pray for Peer Relationships" from the Appendix
Pardon–Micah 7:18
Protection–John 16:33
Purpose–Proverbs 28:5

Chapter 7: Pastor's Family

Read about Eli's family problems in 1 Samuel 2:12, 17, 22–25 and 1 Samuel 4:17–21. Compare and contrast this to Exodus 2:1–9, where another family was in trouble.

Use the Five Ps to pray.

Praise–Psalm 106:1–2
Provision–"Prayer for Pastor's Family" from the Appendix
Pardon–Isaiah 55:7
Protection–2 Samuel 22:3
Purpose–Proverbs19:21

Chapter 8: Physical and Emotional Health

What health issues have you witnessed in pastors and their families? Some issues can be mysterious like the one mentioned in 2 Corinthians 12:7–9. Do you know a minister or a member of the pastoral family who remains ill but lacks a diagnosis?

Other problems are obvious and devastating with no known cure but to cry out to God for healing (see Dan. 4:33–34).

For this session, use the word *pray* to intercede for our pastors.

PRAY is an acronym for these functions: Praise God for his glorious work, his character, and his grace; Request God's providence for Kingdom concerns and for the needs for others; Ask God for the things you need; Yield to his Lordship in your life and rest in it.

Praise–Revelation 4:11
Request–"Persevering Prayer" from the Appendix

Ask–Ephesians 6:18

Yield–Romans 6:13

Chapter 9: Pit Stop for Burnout

On a three-by-five-inch card, explain the process of a battery going dead. Did it happen all at once or gradually?

Have you ever experienced burnout? Possibly, the most burned out person in the Bible is found lamenting in Jeremiah 20:7–10. What are some issues that led to his weariness and depression? Use PRAY to intercede for your minister.

Praise–Isaiah 37:16

Request–"Persevering Prayer" from the Appendix

Ask–Matthew 7:7

Yield–Proverbs 3:5–6

Chapter 10: The Pain of Moral Issues and Forced Exits

In a group of two or three, develop a definition of conflict that does not contain a negative term. Share your definition with the entire group. Was this a difficult exercise? Why or why not? Does the world and the church view conflict differently? If so, in what way?

In Acts 15:1–11, what was the disagreement and how was this dispute settled?

In Acts 15:36–40, what was the conflict and how was this clash settled?

Use the PRAY method for prayer time.

Praise–Psalm 9:1–2, Jeremiah 32:27

Request–"Persevering Prayer" from the Appendix

Ask–Ephesians 3:20

Yield–James 4:7

Chapter 11: Passing It On

Read Matthew 4:18–22 and discuss how Jesus asked Peter, Andrew, James, and John to follow him.

In John 1:43–46, consider how Jesus asked Phillip to be a disciple and how Phillip asked Nathaniel to follow as well. When Nathaniel questioned Phillip, what was Phillip's response?

Can you use these same methods to invite people in your church to join you in praying for your pastor?

Using the ACTS acronym, pray about recruiting members to join you. Remember ACTS stands for Adoration, Confession, Thanksgiving, and Supplication.

A–Ephesians 1:3, Galatians 1:3–5

C–Jeremiah 17:9–10

T–2 Thessalonians 1:3

S–"Prayers for Passing It On" from the Appendix

ABOUT THE AUTHOR

Sally U. Smith's writing career began during summer vacation in her junior high years. Friends wrote her letters of what they were doing. She compiled and typed them (using a manual typewriter and carbon paper), then mailed the newsletter to her friends.

Along with her pastor's wife several years ago, she formed a group to pray for her pastor during his sermon. The prayer lists in the Appendix are from those prayer sessions. She remains a faithful member of the prayer team in her church.

Sally U. Smith has written over one hundred articles for magazines such as *The Standard*, *Vista*, *The Lookout*, *Live!*, and *Club House, Jr.* She contributed to four anthologies: *Cup of Comfort Devotional for Mothers*, *Along the Way for Teens*, *Extraordinary Answers to Prayers*, and *101 Facets of Faith*. In addition, Smith has written numerous articles and submitted a number of photographs to her hometown newspaper.

Smith is a sought after speaker for adults and teens. Her speaking topics cover prayer, leadership, and parenting at conferences, retreats, workshops, seminars, banquets, teas, and other events.

She has a B.A. in psychology and an M.Ed. in counseling. Smith taught math and computers for twelve years before serving as a guidance counselor for seven years. In her community, she also taught parenting classes.

From southwest Missouri, Smith has been married for over forty years and has one biological, four foster, and two adopted children.

///

Get your prayer up to speed

///

Pray to Win

If you like to pray and see God answer,
then watch for more books in this powerful series.

I lay my requests before you and wait expectantly.
Psalm 5:3

NOTES

Introduction

1.	A. Larry Ross, "We Lost Another 'Giant' of the Faith," *Assist News Service*, January 26, 2017, http://bit.ly/2qxdd9h (accessed January 26, 2017).

Chapter 1

2.	William Burt, *Stock Car Race Fan's Reference Guide: Understanding NASCAR* (Osceola, WI: MBI Publishing, 1999), 148–152.

3.	Timothy Miller and Steve Milton, *NASCAR Now!* (Buffalo, NY: Firefly Books, 2006), 34–35.

4.	Staff Writer, "Daytona II: Dodge – Rusty Wallace Interview," *motorsport.com*, https://www.motorsport.com/nascar-cup/news/daytona-ii-dodge-rusty-wallace-interview/ (accessed April 17, 2017).

5.	Barna Group, *The State of Pastors* (Ventura, CA: Barna Books, 2017), 25–26.

6.   C. Peter Wagner, *Prayer Shield* (Ventura, CA: Regal Books, 1992), 19.
7.   E. M. Bounds, *The Complete Works of E.M. Bounds on Prayer* (Grand Rapids, MI: Baker Book House, 1990), 423.
8.   "How to Pray for Your Pastor" *worldnetworkof prayer. com*, http://bit.ly/2r1SW7S (accessed April 17, 2017).

Chapter 2
9.   "Hendrick Motorsports," *Hendrick Motorsports, Inc.*, http://bit.ly/2r7g1cT (accessed April 17, 2017).
10.   Joanne Mattern, *Behind Every Great Driver*, (Jefferson City, MO: Children's Press, 2007), 22.
11.   "Greg Biffle" *Wikipedia, https://en.wikipedia.org/wiki/ Greg_Biffle* (accessed April 17, 2017).
12.   Joanne Mattern, *Behind Every Great Driver*, (Jefferson City, MO: Children's Press, 2007), 35.
13.   Water, *Encyclopedia of Christian Quotations*, 772.
14.   Andrew Murray, *With Christ in the School of Prayer*, (Uhrichsville, OH: Barbour Publishing, Inc., 2005), 147.
15.   Mark Martin, *NASCAR for Dummies,* 2nd ed. (Indianapolis: Wiley Publishing, 2005), 143–144.
16.   Bob Roberts, Tunde Bolanta, and others, "Engaging the Enemy" *Leadership Journal*, http://bit.ly/2s5qVNc (accessed March 7, 2013).
17.   Chris Turner, "Terminations: 1,300 staff dismissed in 2005," *Facts & Trends* 53 (2007): 39.

Chapter 3
18.   "Richard Petty", *Wikipedia*, http://en.wikipedia.org/wiki/ Richard_Petty (accessed on May 6, 2011).

19. Mark Martin, *NASCAR for Dummies, 2nd ed.* (Indianapolis: Wiley Publishing, 2005), 95–100.
20. H. B. London, Jr., "I See That Hand: What Do You See as Your Number One Priority?" *The Parsonage*, August 25, 2001.
21. H. B. London, Jr. and Neil B. Wiseman, *Pastors at Risk*, (Wheaton, IL.: Victor Books, 1993), 179.
22. Craig Groeschel, *Confessions of a Pastor*, (Sisters, OR: Multnomah Publishers, 2006), 11.
23. Liz Allison, *The Girl's Guide to NASCAR* (New York: Center Street, 2006), 39.
24. Terry C. Muck, "10 Questions about the Devotional Life," *Leadership Journal*, Winter 1982, 30–39.
25. Water, *Encyclopedia of Christian Quotations*, 772.
26. "Aiden Wilson Tozer," *Wikipedia*, http://en.wikipedia. org/wiki/A.W._Tozer (accessed on July 5, 2007).
27. Richard P. Hansen with David Wall, "Why People Don't Pray: It May Not Be the Reasons We Think," *Leadership Journal*, Fall 1994, 61–63.
28. Thom Rainer, "Prayer and Healthy Churches," *Facts and Trends,* Spring 2011, 4–5.

Chapter 4
29. Staff Writer, "Kentucky Speedway Traffic Debacle Remembered," *foxsports.com*, http://foxs.pt/2rHIIh4 (accessed April 17, 2017).
30. John Maxwell, *Partners in Prayer*, (Nashville, TN: Thomas Nelson, 1996), 79.
31. Mark Martin, *NASCAR for Dummies,* 2nd ed. (Indianapolis: Wiley Publishing, 2005), 103–107.

32. "A Profile of Protestant Pastors in Anticipation of 'Pastor Appreciation Month,'" *barna.com*, September 25, 2001, http://bit.ly/2r79RJC (accessed October 3, 2006).

33. Trevor Lee, "My Rookie Season—What I Learned in My First Year As a Pastor," *Leadership Journal*, Winter 2011, http://bit.ly/2qXSoD6 (accessed May 10, 2011).

34. Jack Connell, "Ministry Mulligans—If I had it to do all over again . . ." *Leadership Journal*, Spring 2011, http://bit.ly/2rqfzqV (May 11, 2011).

35. Barna Group, *The State of Pastors* (Ventura, CA: Barna Books, 2017), 65–67.

36. Robin Sigars, email message to author, May 11, 2011.

37. John Ortberg, "A *Rev!* Interview with John Ortberg," *Rev!*, May/June, 2006.

38. Pete Scazzero, "Skimming – Stop Trying to Look Good, and Do the Dirty Work Beneath the Surface," *Leadership*, Winter, 2009. http://bit.ly/2qXQbaw (accessed May 11, 2011).

39. Jack Connell, "Ministry Mulligans—If I had it to do all over again . . ." *Leadership Journal*, Spring 2011, http://bit.ly/2qkWHcJ (accessed May 11, 2011).

40. Pete Scazzero, "Skimming—Stop Trying to Look Good, and Do the Dirty Work beneath the Surface," *Leadership Journal*, Winter 2009, http://bit.ly/2qoHVxF (accessed May 11, 2011).

41. Robin Sigars, email message to author, May 11, 2011.

42. Warren Bennis and Burt Nanus, *Leaders: Strategies for Taking Charge* (New York: HarperCollins, 1997), 4.

43. Henry and Richard Blackaby, *Spiritual Leadership* (Nashville, TN: Broadman & Holman, 2001), 20.

44. Mike Huckabee, *Character Is the Issue* (Nashville, TN: Broadman & Holman, 1997), 105–106.

45. Rick Rusaw, "Get Out!" *Rev!*, May/June, 2008, 58-64.

46. Pat Valeriano, "A Survey of Ministers Wives," *Leadership Journal*, Fall 1981, http://bit.ly/2r5C8y6 (accessed May 11, 2011).

47. Bob Schmidgall, "Good Pastor, Good Parent," *Leadership Journal*, Summer 1994, http://bit.ly/2qXRh68 (accessed May 11, 2011).

48. Pete Scazzero, "Skimming".

49. Liz Allison, *The Girl's Guide to NASCAR* (New York: Center Street, 2006), 36.

50. Lorna Dobson, *Caring for Your Pastor: Helping God's Servant to Minister with Joy* (Grand Rapids, MI: Kregel Publications, 2001), 64–65.

Chapter 5

51. Leith Anderson, *Dying for Change* (Grand Rapids, MI: Bethany House, 1998), 177.

52. The Barna Group, "Most American Christians Do Not Believe that Satan or the Holy Spirit Exist," *barna.com*, April 10, 2009, http://bit.ly/2qsAogr (accessed June 2, 2011).

53. Rick Warren, "Spiritual Warfare in Ministry," *Fresno Pacific University Campus Blogs*, January 26, 2017, http://bit.ly/2qso6Vu (accessed April 17, 2017).

54. Daily Christian Quote website, http://bit.ly/2qle2lM (accessed May 18, 2011).

55. Barna Group, *The State of Pastors* (CA: Barna Books, 2017), 20–22.

56. Forum, "Facing the Wreckage of Evil" interview with Earl Palmer, *Leadership Journal*, October 1, 1986, http://bit.ly/2rqAEBN (accessed May 11, 2011).

57. Forum, "Facing the Wreckage of Evil" interview with Harold Bussell, *Leadership Journal*, October 1, 1986, http://bit.ly/2rqAEBN (accessed May 11, 2011).

58. "David Koresh," *Wikipedia*, http://en.wikipedia.org/wiki/David_Koresh (accessed June 8, 2011).

59. "Jim Jones," *Wikipedia*, http://en.wikipedia.org/wiki/Jim_Jones (accessed June 8, 2011).

60. Tom Breen, "End of Days in May? Believers Enter Final Stretch," NBCNews.com, January 3, 2011, http://nbcnews.to/2qV8xtH (accessed March 31, 2017).

61. Neil Graves and Lukas I. Alpert, "World Will End on May 21 Says Ex-MTA Worker Robert Fitzpatrick, Who's Putting Money Where Mouth Is," *New York Daily News*, May 12, 2011.

62. Liz Allison, *The Girl's Guide to NASCAR* (New York: Center Street, 2006), 81.

63. Hannah Whitall Smith, *A Christian's Secret of a Happy Life* (New Kensington, PA: Whitaker House, 1983), 91–92.

64. Neil T. Anderson, *The Bondage Breaker* (Eugene, OR: Harvest House, 1993), 166.

65. Mark Martin, *NASCAR for Dummies,* 2nd ed. (Indianapolis: Wiley Publishing, 2005), 152, 155.

66. Mark Roberts, Tunde Bolanta and others, "Engaging the Enemy," *Leadership Journal*, Spring 2012, http://bit.ly/2s5qVNc (accessed March 7, 2013).

67. Neil T. Anderson, *T-H-E Bondage Breaker* (Eugene, OR: Harvest House, 1993), 143.

68. Merrill F. Unger, *What Demons Can Do to Saints* (Chicago: Moody Press, 1977), 51.
69. H. B. London Jr., "Pornography: A Very Real and Troublesome Problem," *The Parsonage*, June 1994.
70. Billy Graham, *Just As I Am* (New York: HarperCollins, 1997), 332–333.
71. Ibid., 326, 333.
72. Allison, *Girl's*, 70.
73. Roger Barrier, "When the Force Is Against You," *Leadership Journal*, January 1, 1999, http://bit.ly/2ql7cg3 (accessed June 8, 2011).
74. Vernon Maxted, personal letter to author, May 12, 2011.
75. Debbie Moore, "Piper Says Prayer is Essential in Battling Spiritual Warfare," *Baptist Press*, October 9, 2000, http://bit.ly/2ql7cg3 (accessed May 23, 2011).

Chapter 6
76. The auto editors of *Consumer Guide*, "Red Byron," *How Stuff Works*, http://bit.ly/2r6Xygj (accessed June 29, 2011).
77. "Red Byron," *Wikipedia*, http://en.wikipedia.org/wiki/Red_Byron (accessed June 29, 2011).
78. Ryan McGee, "'Byron Was Great Champion, Veteran," *espn.com*, http://es.pn/2qY2io8 (accessed November 10, 2012).
79. "Red Byron," *nascar.com*, February 20, 2015, http://nas.cr/2qXRVRg (accessed June 29, 2015).
80. Ibid.
81. "Raymond Parks (auto racing)," *Wikipedia*, http://en.wikipedia.org/wiki/Raymond_Parks_(car_owner) (accessed July 5, 2011).

82. "The NASCAR Founding Meeting December 14, 1947 at the Streamline Hotel in Daytona Beach, FL," *HistoryChannel.com*, http://bit.ly/2rquaTp (accessed July 5, 2011).

83. Neal Thompson, *Driving with the Devil* (New York: Crown Publishers, 2006), 332, 349.

84. "Pastors Feel Confident in Ministry, But Many Struggle in their Interaction with Others," *barna.com*, July 10, 2006, http://bit.ly/2qXLgGt (accessed May 11, 2011).

85. John Ortberg, "Spiritual Friends," *Leadership Journal*, April 14, 2008, http://bit.ly/2qsEwx3 (accessed July 8, 2011).

86. William Richard Ezell, "The Matter of Integrity," *The Parsonage,* 2003.

87. H. B. London Jr., "The Little Black Book: A Lesson in Forgiveness," *Pastor to Pastor*, September/October, 1999.

88. Ortberg, "Spiritual Friends."

89. Clark Cothern, "Light in Your Eyes," *Leadership Journal*, Winter 2011, http://bit.ly/2r5vNCX (accessed May 18, 2011).

90. Gordon MacDonald, *Renewing Your Spiritual Passion* (Nashville, TN: Thomas Nelson, 1989), 187.

91. Timothy Miller, *NASCAR Now!* (Richmond Hill, ON: Firefly Books, 2006), 139.

92. Ibid., 142.

93. Ron Edmondson, "How My Personal Prayer Team Is Structured," *ChurchLeaders,* June 8, 2012, http://bit.ly/2qoUYPN (accessed April 23, 2013).

94. Dietrich Bonhoeffer, *Life Together*, trans. John Doberstein (New York: Harper & Row, 1954), 86.

95. MacDonald, *Renewing Your Spiritual Passion*, 193.
96. Ralph N. Paulk, "McMurray, Montoya Likely Draft Partners," *TRIBLive*, February 18, 2011, http://bit.ly/2rI685M (accessed June 30, 2013).
97. Mark Water, comp., *The New Encyclopedia of Christian Quotations* (Grand Rapids, MI: Baker Book House, 2000), 306.
98. Jerry B. Jenkins, "George Beverly Shea: A Man of Surprising Humor," *Assist News Service*, April 19, 2013, http://bit.ly/2qoEWoT (accessed April 19, 2013).
99. H. B. London Jr., "Mentoring," *Pastor to Pastor*, February 1995.
100. Gordon MacDonald, "When Bad Things Happen to Good Relationships," *Leadership Journal*, Winter 2011, http://bit.ly/2qsrf7K (accessed July 8, 2011).
101. Sharon Predovich, "Overcoming the Obstacles to Women in Ministry," *Ministry Today*, March/April, 2003.
102. MacDonald, *Renewing Your Spiritual Passion*, 178.
103. Sporting News Wire Service, "Ten Years Ago … an Emotional Win for Junior," *NASCAR.com*, June 29, 2011, http://nas.cr/2r7oxs4 (accessed July 16, 2011).
104. Ibid.

Chapter 7
105. Timothy Miller, *NASCAR Now!* (Richmond Hill, Ont.: Firefly Books, 2006), 154–155.
106. "Bob Flock," *Wikipedia*, http://en.wikipedia.org/wiki/Bob Flock (accessed July 15, 2013).
107. "Fonty Flock," *Wikipedia*, http://en.wikipedia.org/wiki/Fonty Flock (accessed July 15, 2013).

108. "Tim Flock," *Wikipedia*, http://en.wikipedia.org/wiki/ Tim Flock (accessed July 15, 2013).
109. "Ethel Mobley," *Wikipedia*, http://en.wikipedia.org/wiki/ Ethel Mobley (accessed July 15, 2013).
110. Miller, *NASCAR Now!*, 154.
111. "Fonty Flock," *Memim Encyclopedia*, https://memim. com/fonty-flock.html (accessed July 15, 2013).
112. "Bob Flock," *Wikipedia*.
113. Christine Hoover, "7 Lies Ministry Wives Believe," *ChurchLeaders*, May 30, 2013, http://bit.ly/2qY4CLZ (accessed June 6, 2013).
114. Thom Rainer, "What Pastors' Wives Wish They Knew Before," *ChurchLeaders*, May 21, 2013, http://bit. ly/2qsXqUw (accessed May 22, 2013).
115. Pat Valeriano, "A Survey of Minsters Wives," *Leadership Journal*, Fall 1981, http://bit.ly/2r5C8y6 (accessed May 18, 2011).
116. Jane Rubietta, "The High Chair Day," *The Parsonage*, November 2002, http://bit.ly/2qoLW5d (accessed May 21, 2011).
117. Joyce Williams, comp., *She Can't Even Play the Piano!: Insights for Ministry Wives* (Kansas City, MO: Beacon Hill Press, 2005), 26.
118. Oswald Chambers, *My Utmost for His Highest Journal* (Uhrichsville, OH: Barbour, 1963).
119. "Columbia International University," *Wikipedia*, http:// en.wikipedia.org/wiki/Columbia International University (accessed July 18, 2013).
120. Summer Bethea, "Love and Alzheimer's," *The Parsonage*, 2005, http://bit.ly/2ql5E5S (accessed May 21, 2011).

121. Sarah Eekhoff Zylstra, "Died: Robertson McQuilkin, College President Praised for Alzheimer's Resignation," *Christianity Today, June 2, 2016,* http://bit.ly/1P8K6e2 (accessed July 18, 2016).
122. Lorna Dobson, *I'm More Than the Pastor's Wife* (Grand Rapids: Zondervan Publishing House, 1995), 122.
123. Williams, *Can't Even Play the Piano*,18.
124. Donna Alder, "How to Encourage Your Pastor's Wife," *The Parsonage*, http://bit.ly/2s5yjIF (accessed May 21, 2011).
125. Williams, *Can't Even Play the Piano*, 20.
126. Macel Falwell, *Jerry Falwell: His Life and Legacy* (New York: Howard Books, 2008), 59.
127. Valeriano, "Survey of Ministry Wives."
128. Frank Schaefer, "Self-Care Tips for the Clergy Family," *Desperate Preacher*, http://bit.ly/2r7hSOQ (accessed May 23, 2011).
129. Diane Langberg, *Counsel for Pastors' Wives* (Grand Rapids, MI: Zondervan, 1988), 16.
130. Willie E. Hucks II, "The Life of the Pastoral Family: An Interview with Willie and Elaine Oliver," *Ministry*, March 2013, 6-9.
131. "About Jeff Gordon," *jeffgordon.com*, http://bit. ly/1NVGgK4 (accessed April 19, 2017).
132. Sandra McKee, "Cause of Gordon Split May Best Remain Private," *Baltimore Sun*, March 24, 2002, http:// bit.ly/2s5BgZt (accessed July 21, 2011).
133. "Jeff Gordon's Christian Testimony," *MRO Motor Racing Outreach*, 2015, http://bit.ly/2qY57pe (accessed April 18, 2017).

134. Barna Group, *The State of Pastors* (Ventura, CA: Barna Books, 2017), 34–36.
135. Colleen Evans, "Friends: A Minister's Wife Can Find Them in the Strangest Places – Like Church," *The Parsonage*, http://bit.ly/2qoqZr6 (accessed May 21, 2011).
136. Langberg, *Counsel for Pastors' Wives*, 67–68.
137. Valeriano, "Survey of Ministry Wives."
138. Dobson, *I'm More Than the Pastor's Wife*, 79–80.
139. Muriel Phillips, "On Being Mrs. Pastor," *Ministry*, October 1984, http://bit.ly/2rI9sOp (accessed June 30, 2013).
140. Mary E. Bess, *Tips for Ministers and Mates* (Nashville, TN: Broadman Press, 1987), 38–39.
141. Falwell, *Jerry Falwell,* 202–206.
142. Alder, "Encourage Your Pastor's Wife."
143. Nancy Pannell, *Being a Minister's Wife and Being Yourself* (Nashville, TN: Broadman Press, 1993), 141–142.
144. Terry W. Dorsett, *Developing Leadership Teams in the Bivocational Church* (Bloomington, IN: CrossBooks, 2010), 1–3.
145. Susan Stevens, "Bivocational Battle Plan," *The Parsonage*, http://bit.ly/2r5ztV2 (accessed May 21, 2011).
146. Kristi Rector, "Working Women: Pastors' Wives with Other Titles", *The Parsonage*, http://bit.ly/2rqmH6F (accessed May 21, 2011).
147. Williams, *Can't Even Play the Piano,* 47.
148. Langberg, *Counsel for Pastors' Wives*, 48–49.
149. Dobson, *Caring for Your Pastor*, 109.

150. Williams, *Can't Even Play the Piano*, 106.
151. Dobson, *Caring for Your Pastor*, 110–111.
152. Jeana Floyd, *10 Things Every Minister's Wife Needs to Know* (Green Forest, AR: New Leaf Press, 2009), 124.
153. Floyd, *10 Things*, 115–116.
154. Valeriano, "Survey of Minister's Wives."
155. Rainer, "What Pastors' Wives Wish They Knew."
156. Liz Allison, *The Girl's Guide to NASCAR* (New York: Center Street, 2006), 25.
157. Valeriano, "Survey of Minister's Wives."
158. Floyd, *10 Things*, 57.
159. Stephanie Wolfe, "Ministering to the Minister," *The Parsonage*, http://bit.ly/2rI9x4x (accessed May 21, 2011).
160. Joe McKeever, "Why the Pastor's Wife is the MOST Vulnerable Person in Your Church", *Church Leaders*, November 17, 2015, http://bit.ly/2r5Ib5C (accessed September 23, 2013).
161. Jena Fellers, email message to author, July 2, 2013.
162. "David Reutimann," *Wikipedia*, http://en.wikipedia.org/wiki/David Reutimann (accessed October 29, 2013).
163. David Newton, "A dynamic father-son duo", *ESPN.com*, June 6, 2011, http://es.pn/2ql1Jpv (accessed October 29, 2013).
164. Julianna Preble Fife, "Behind the Mask (Part 1)," *The Parsonage*, http://bit.ly/2qkVzWK (accessed May 20, 2011).
165. Franklin Graham, *Rebel with a Cause* (Nashville: Thomas Nelson, 1995), 1.

166. Kyle Idleman, "The Spotlight Syndrome", *Leadership Journal*, Spring 2008, http://bit.ly/2qkVzWK (accessed June 20, 2008).

167. Joe McKeever, "You MUST Take the Preacher's Kids Out of the Crosshairs," *ChurchLeaders*, September 30, 2013, http://bit.ly/2qsMTsi (accessed October 7, 2013).

168. Carole Brousson Anderson, "Pastors' Kids: in and out", *Ministry*, May 1996, 14-15.

169. Graham, *Rebel with a Cause,* 58.

170. Chonda Pierce, *Second Row, Piano Side* (Kansas City, MO: Beacon Hill Press, 1996), 13–17, 23–26, 50–55, 58-60, 64–65, 75–81.

171. Kristin Asimakoupoulos, "Not so Bad after All", *Just Between Us*, Spring 2008, 28–29.

172. George Stahnke, "PKs and the Pressure of Ministry," *Thriving Pastor*, http://bit.ly/2qoQjNy (accessed August 27, 2013).

173. Todd and Jedd Hafer, *Snickers from the Front Pew* (Tulsa, OK: Honor Books, 2000), 161–162.

Chapter 8

174. "Trevor Bayne," *Wikipedia*, http://en.wikipedia.org/wiki/Trevor_Bayne (accessed June 12, 2014).

175. David Caraviello, "Trevor Bayne Diagnosed with Multiple Sclerosis," *NASCAR.com*, November 12, 2013, http://nas.cr/2s2aIJs (accessed November 12, 2013).

176. Mark Hensch, "Is Trevor Bayne NASCAR's Tim Tebow?" *The Christian Post*, December 22, 2011, http://bit.ly/2quWvTF (accessed June 12, 2014).

177. Terry Dorsett, "Victory over Cancer and the Will of God," *Next Generation Evangelistic Network*, April 9, 2014, http://bit.ly/2s8EFH7 (accessed April 9, 2014).

178. Terry Dorsett, April 1, 2014 and March 31, 2014, http://bit.ly/2qquD3K (accessed April 1, 2014).

179. Terry Dorsett, "Victory over Cancer and the Will of God," *Next Generation Evangelistic Network*, April 9, 2014, http://bit.ly/2s8EFH7 (accessed April 9, 2014).

180. "Charles Finney," *Christianity Today.com* http://bit.ly/2r8rlU0 (accessed July 24, 2014).

181. "Charles Grandison Finney," http://en.wikipedia.org/wiki/Charles_Grandison_Finney, (accessed July 23).

182. Ed Dobson, "Ed's Story," http://edsstory.com, (accessed April 18, 2014).

183. "Charles Spurgeon," *Wikipedia*, http://en.wikipedia.org/wiki/Charles_Spurgeon (accessed March 23, 2015).

184. Randy Alcorn, "Third (and Final) on Spurgeon, Ministry and Depression," *Eternal Perspective Ministries Blog*, September 17, 2007, http://bit.ly/2r08KLk (accessed March 23, 2015).

185. Toni Ridgaway, "Pastor Commits Suicide While Congregation Waits for Him to Preach," *ChurchLeaders*, November 14, 2013, http://bit.ly/2qqo9ly (accessed November 22, 2013).

186. J. R. Briggs, "Transforming Failure: How God Used a Painful Season of Ministry to Change My Life," *Leadership Journal*, Spring 2014, 24.

187. Art Greco, "Attacked by a Monster," *Leadership Journal*, Spring 2009, http://bit.ly/2r7Lqda (accessed May 19, 2011).

188. David Trig, "High Anxiety," *Leadership Journal*, Summer 2004, http://bit.ly/XA6Qim (accessed October 9, 2014).

189. Tommy Nelson, "Anxiety Attack!" *Leadership Journal*, Winter 2013, http://bit.ly/2qqZUmW (accessed February 20, 2013).

190. Nicola Menzie, "Pastor Ron Carpenter Reveals Wife's Mental Illness, Adultery in Heart-Wrenching Sunday Confession," *Christian Post*, October 14, 2013, http://bit.ly/2s8CinI (accessed October 25, 2014); and Jennifer LeClaire, "After Multiple Affairs, Pastor Ron Carpenter's Wife Seeks Psychiatric Treatment," *Charisma News*, October 14, 2013, http://bit.ly/2r86Oi4 (accessed February 23, 2015).

191. Nicola Menzie, "Pastor Ron Carpenter's Wife, Hope, Returns to SC Megachurch as He Rebukes Christian Leaders Who Supported His Desire for Divorce," *Christian Post*, February 17, 2014, http://bit.ly/1hqhalT (accessed February 23, 2015).

192. Name Withheld, "When My Daughter Said, 'I'm gay'," *Leadership Journal*, 2014, http://bit.ly/2fSKofc (accessed May 6, 2014).

193. "Davey Allison," *Wikipedia*, http://en.wikipedia.org/wiki/Davey_Allison (accessed January 12, 2007).

194. Liz Allison, *The Girl's Guide to NASCAR* (New York: Center Street, 2006), xx-xxi.

195. Piers Morgan, "Interview with Rick and Kay Warren," *Piers Morgan Live*, September 17, 2013, http://cnn.it/2qnp0aB (accessed October 1, 2013).

196. "Kübler-Ross model," *Wikipedia*, http://en.wikipedia.org/wiki/Kübler-Ross model (accessed March 23, 2015).

197. Rick and Kay Warren, "How to Get Through What You're Going Through," Saddleback Church Media, http://bit.ly/1NEHtQr (accessed March 23, 2015); and Morgan, "Interview with Rick and Kay Warren."

198. John E. Colwell, "Befriending the Darkness," *Leadership Journal*, January 2013, http://bit.ly/2qnBf6O (accessed March 7, 2013).

Chapter 9

199. "Jeremy Mayfield," *Racing-Reference.Info*, http://www.racing-reference.info/driver/Jeremy_Mayfield (accessed May 11, 2015).

200. Dave Faherty, "Jeremy Mayfield's $1.8M Mansion to Be Burned Down," *WSOCTV.com*, December 11, 2013, http://on.wsoctv.com/1fnxYp4 (accessed May 11, 2015).

201. "Ex-NASCAR Driver Jeremy Mayfield Convicted, Fined," *USA Today*, January 7, 2014, https://usat.ly/2rMD25k (accessed May 7, 2015).

202. J. R. Briggs, "Transforming Failure: How God Used a Painful Season of Ministry to Change My Life," *Leadership Journal*, Spring 2014, 20–24.

203. C. E., "It's Not Fun Anymore," *PastorBurnout.com*, http://bit.ly/2sblk83 (accessed May 11, 2015).

204. S. J., "The Jonah Effect," *PastorBurnout.com*, http://bit.ly/2rLSBdK (accessed May 11, 2015).

205. Brian Howard, "4 Incredibly Simple Steps to Avoid Burnout," *ChurchLeaders,* July 4, 2014, http://bit.ly/2sbyAtH (accessed May 10, 2015).

206. Ulrich Kraft, "Burned Out," *Scientific American Mind*, June/July 2006, 28–33.

207. Wayne Cordeiro, *Leading on Empty: Refilling Your Tank and Renewing Your Passion,* (Minneapolis: Bethany House, 2009), 23.
208. Southwest Pastor, "Where Do I Go from Here?" *PastorBurnout.com,* http://bit.ly/2raMJrM (accessed May 11, 2015).
209. Rick Warren, "Four Big Mistakes that Lead to Ministry Burnout," *Pastors.com,* May 30, 2014, http://bit.ly/2rarPbX (accessed May 30, 2014).
210. Sean Fowlds, "Drop the Juggling Act: Coping with Busyness without Burning Out," *Facts & Trends,* March/April, 2015, 36–37.
211. US Pastor, "Death by Pastor Burnout," *PastorBurnout.com,* http://bit.ly/2r2vMRI (accessed May 11, 2015).
212. Barna Group, *The State of Pastors,* (Ventura, CA: Barna Books, 2017), 100.
213. Thom Rainer, "12 Ways Pastors Went from Burnout to Vision," *ChurchLeaders,* April 27, 2015, http://bit.ly/2s4K2rO (accessed August 12, 2015).
214. Cordeiro, *Leading on Empty,* 57.
215. Kevin Conklin, "Facing Your Board with a Difficulty," *ThrivingPastor.com,* http://bit.ly/2raR7XP (accessed May 25, 2015).
216. Cordeiro, *Leading on Empty,* 143–144.
217. Rainer, "12 Ways Pastors Went from Burnout to Vision."
218. Greg Taylor, "When Church Becomes a Pastor's Idol: A *Leadership Journal* Interview with Craig Groeschel and Kyle Idleman," *Leadership Journal,* Spring 2015, http://bit.ly/2r2pNwm (accessed May 25, 2015).
219. Rainer, "12 Ways Pastors Went from Burnout to Vision."
220. Ibid.

221. Taylor, "When Church Becomes a Pastor's Idol."
222. Rainer, "12 Ways Pastors Went from Burnout to Vision."
223. Cordeiro, *Leading on Empty,* 143.
224. Rainer, "12 Ways Pastors Went from Burnout to Vision."
225. Taylor, "When Church Becomes a Pastor's Idol."
226. Rainer, "12 Ways Pastors Went from Burnout to Vision."
227. Cordeiro, *Leading on Empty*, 109.
228. Rainer, "12 Ways Pastors Went from Burnout to Vision."
229. Cordeiro, *Leading on Empty*, 86.
230. Rainer, "12 Ways Pastors Went from Burnout to Vision."
231. Ibid.
232. Ibid.
233. Bob Pockrass, "Jimmie Johnson Wins at Texas for the Seventh Time," *ESPN.com,* April 9, 2017, http://es.pn/2nYCiFi (accessed April 20, 2017).
234. Julie Pierce, "How to Beat Burnout," *Todays Christian Woman,* June 24, 2015, http://bit.ly/2rvlwTn (accessed April 21, 2017).
235. Ibid.
236. Cordeiro, *Leading on Empty,* 122.
237. Ibid., 125.
238. Andrew McMillian, "My Church, My Assassin: When a Glorious Calling Becomes a Silent Killer," *Leadership Journal,* June 24, 2015, http://bit.ly/2s4suMf, (accessed July 5, 2015).
239. Rainer, "12 Ways Pastors Went from Burnout to Vision."
240. Ron Edmondson, "7 Reasons I Need to Regularly Exercise as a Leader," *ChurchLeaders,* July 17, 2015, http://bit.ly/2qpZz8e (accessed August 28, 2015).
241. Miranda Vande Kuyt, "Preventing Burnout for Pastors' Wives. Seven Signs of Stress and How to Prevent It,"

March 27, 2012, http://bit.ly/2qsWccz (accessed April 12, 2017).

242. Erin Wheeler, "Battling Burnout as a Pastor's Wife," March 14, 2017, http://bit.ly/2qq6Apt (accessed April 12, 2017).

243. Quoted in Ken Sande, "Pastors' Wives Can Burn Out Too," June 19, 2016, http://bit.ly/2s4sfkl (accessed April 12, 2017).

244. Quoted in Kevin A. Miller, "Irritating Stereotypes That Make Me a Better Pastor," *Leadership Journal*, Spring 2014, 25–27.

Chapter 10

245. "Aaron Fike," *Wikipedia*, https://en.wikipedia.org/wiki/Aaron_Fike (accessed September 29, 2015).

246. John Lee, "NASCAR Driver Admits to Using Heroin Before Racing," *Choose Help*, April 10, 2008, http://bit.ly/2rvedv3 (accessed September 29,2015).

247. Ryan McGee, "Former Truck Racer Fike Admits Using Heroin on Race Days," *ESPN.com*, April 8, 2008, http://es.pn/2rdbHc5 (accessed September 29, 2015).

248. Bob Pockrass, "Driver Aaron Fike Reinstated: Heroin Use Spurred NASCAR's Drug-Testing Policy," *Sporting News*, August 21, 2012, http://bit.ly/2rdbVzI (accessed September 29, 2015).

249. John W. Kennedy, "Surprised by Addiction," *Leadership Journal*, Spring 2011, http://bit.ly/2raGnbD (accessed June 6, 2011).

250. Ibid.

251. Luke Gilkerson, "Enslaved to Porn: Why I Returned Again and Again to Pornography," *ChurchLeaders*,

October 10, 2013, http://bit.ly/2rb5yLq (accessed October 12, 2013). The blog *Covenant Eyes* is found at http://www.covenanteyes.com.

252. Kennedy, "Surprised by Addiction."

253. Pastor Who's Been There, "Dancing on the Edge," *Parsonage.org*, http://bit.ly/2sblcWb (accessed May 20, 2011).

254. John Ortberg, J. R. Briggs, Mandy Smith, Lee Eclov, Derek Rishmawy, "When One of Us Falls," *Leadership Journal*, June 2015, http://bit.ly/2r2zKtz (accessed July 5, 2015).

255. Darrel Rowland, "Three Stories One Problem," *Christian Standard*, November, 2007, 709–710.

256. "Porn in the Church," *CovenantEyes.com*, 2015, http://bit.ly/1n0WHFM (accessed November 16, 2015).

257. T. C. Ryan, "Where Lust Leads," *Leadership Journal*, Fall 2013, http://bit.ly/2qtbxKa (accessed November 19, 2013).

258. Ibid.

259. H. B. London, Jr., "Pornography: A Very Real and Troublesome Problem," *Parsonage.org*, http://bit.ly/2s53zsa (accessed May 20, 2011).

260. KCTV Staff Writer, "Pastor Admits to Ripping Off Several Landlords," *KCTV5News.com*, June 12, 2013, http://bit.ly/2rd7GnR (accessed June 22, 2013).

261. Esther Laurie, "New Orleans Pastor Commits Suicide After Found on Ashley Madison," September 9, 2015, *ChurchLeaders*, http://bit.ly/2qsR7kH (accessed September 11, 2015).

262. "Ashley Madison Hackers Post Millions of Customer Names," *CNN Money*, August 19, 2015, http://cnnmon. ie/1gWaexQ (accessed September 11, 2015).

263. "Ashley Madison," *Wikipedia.org*, https://en.wikipedia. org/wiki/Ashley_Madison (accessed October 9, 2015).

264. Ed Stetzer, "My Pastor Is on the Ashley Madison List," *Christianity Today*, August 27, 2015, http://bit. ly/1KnAHAk (accessed August 31, 2015).

265. Shelly Duffer, "My Healing Community," *Leadership Journal*, Spring 2015, http://bit.ly/2rvmUW3 (accessed June 2, 2015).

266. Toni Ridgaway, "Alabama Pastor Shocks Congregation with Confessions of AIDS Diagnosis, Sex with Members, Drug Use," *ChurchLeaders*, October 9, 2014, http://bit. ly/2rdd1M5 (accessed October 25, 2014).

267. Darrell Brazell, "Breaking Point," *Leadership Journal*, Winter 2011, http://bit.ly/2r2zFpP (accessed May 18, 2011).

268. Dorothy Greco, "Pastoring Your Church through a Leader's Misconduct," *Leadership Journal*, May 2004, http://bit.ly/2qx8Zdg (accessed May 22, 2015).

269. Anonymous Pastor's Wife, "After the Shock," *The Parsonage*, http://bit.ly/2rd8j0L (accessed May 21, 2011).

270. Greco, "Pastoring Your Church through a Leader's Misconduct."

271. Darrel Rowland, "Three Stories One Problem," *Christian Standard*, November, 2007, 708.

272. "5 Things Pastors Should Learn from Josh Duggar's Confession," *ChurchLeaders*, August 20, 2015, http:// bit.ly/2qt7y0i (accessed August 22, 2015).

273. Ed Stetzer, "I'm on the Ashley Madison List. Now What?" *Christianity Today*, August 26, 2016, http://bit. ly/1iwYbrU (accessed August 26, 2015).

274. Greco, "Pastoring Your Church through a Leader's Misconduct."

275. Rowland, "Three Stories One Problem," 709–710.

276. Anonymous Pastor's Wife, "After the Shock."

277. Greco, "Pastoring Your Church through a Leader's Misconduct."

278. Ibid.

279. David Newton, "Danica Patrick's Divorce Official," *ESPN.com*, April 25, 2013, http://es.pn/2qt8n9x (accessed October 29, 2013).

280. Duffer, "My Healing Community."

281. Anonymous Pastor's Wife, "After the Shock."

282. Melody Schilling, "You're Fired!" *The Parsonage*, http:// bit.ly/2qt80vu (accessed May 21, 2011).

283. 283. Duffer, "My Healing Community."

284. "Forced out of Ministry," *National Association of Evangelicals*, July 2015, http://bit.ly/2qt7SMy (accessed October 6, 2015).

285. "Terminations," *Priscilla's Friends*, http://bit. ly/2qq8yWT (accessed November 8, 2015).

286. Mark, "Testimonials," *PastorCare*, http://bit.ly/2rMjyxD (accessed November 9, 2015).

287. "Terminations," *Priscilla's Friends.*

288. David L. Goetz, "Forced Out," *Leadership Journal*, Winter 1996, http://bit.ly/2r2vOsY (accessed November 9, 2015).

289. "Forced out of Ministry," *National Association of Evangelicals.*

290. Charles H. Chandler, "Is There a Rulebook on Forced Terminations?" *Servant* -Ministering to Ministers Foundation, October, 2000, Ministering to Ministers Foundation, Inc., http://bit.ly/2raASd6 (accessed November 8, 2015).

291. Ken Sande, "Strike the Shepherd–Losing Pastors in the Church," Peacemaker Ministries, February 18, 2015, http://bit.ly/2rdn5o0 (accessed November 9, 2015).

292. Dennis Fletcher, "Business as Usual," *Leadership Journal,* Summer 2014, 42.

293. Rodney Crowell, "Spiritual Survival for a Forced Exit," *Leadership Journal*, Winter 1989, http://bit.ly/2rMHyB4 (accessed May 20, 2011).

294. Paul David Tripp, *Dangerous Calling*, (Wheaton, IL: Crossway, 2012) pp. 30–31.

295. Ibid.,131.

296. Shelly Esser, "Grounds for Restoration," *Parsonage.org,* http://bit.ly/2rda3XR (accessed May 21, 2011).

297. "Forced out of Ministry," *National Association of Evangelicals.*

298. Jason Helopoulos, "Pastors Need Your Care–Part I," The Gospel Coalition, June 27, 2013, http://bit.ly/2qxcMaD (accessed October 17, 2016).

Chapter 11

299. Maggie MacKenzie, "Hendrick Motorsports Welcomes New Class of Pit Crew Members," *NASCAR.com*, September 23, 2015, http://nas.cr/2sbBE8Z (accessed January 4, 2017).

300. NASCAR Release, "NASCAR Drive for Diversity Hosts First Pit Crew Combine," *NASCAR.com*, May 27, 2015, http://nas.cr/2s5058Q (accessed January 4, 2017).

301. Stephen and Alex Kendrick, *The Battle Plan for Prayer: From Basic Training to Targeted Strategies*, (Nashville, TN: B&H Publishing Group, 2015), 212–213.

302. Dan Reiland, "Prayer Partners Required," *ChurchLeaders*, September 13, 2015, http://bit.ly/2raBOy8 (accessed January 17, 2017).

303. Barna Group, *The State of Pastors* (Ventura, CA: Barna Books, 2017), 13.

304. Dietrich Bonhoeffer, *Life Together* (New York: Harper Row, 1976), 62.

305. Kenny Bruce, "Horsepower Reduction Among 2015 Rules Package Changes," *NASCAR.com*, September 23, 2014, http://nas.cr/2rdnUgA (accessed January 26, 2017).

306. Kendrick, *Battle Plan*, 18–19.

Morgan James
Speakers Group

We connect Morgan James published authors with live and online events and audiences who will benefit from their expertise.

 Morgan James makes all of our titles available
through the Library for All Charity Organization.

www.LibraryForAll.org